The Tyranny of the Politically Correct - Totalitarianism in the Postmodern Age
by
Keith Preston

The Tyranny of the Politically Correct
- Totalitarianism in the Postmodern Age

by

Keith Preston

ISBN-13: 978-1-910881-16-3

Black House Publishing Ltd
Kemp House
152 City Road
London
UNITED KINGDOM
EC1V 2NX

www.blackhousepublishing.com
Email: info@blackhousepublishing.com

Contents

Introduction

An important transformation has slowly occurred within the Western industrialized democracies since the 1990s. It is a transformation that is now widely recognized, frequently criticized, and often considered to be a source of amusement by many people even as many others seek to deny its reality, or the genuine nature of its underlying implications. The American conservative writer William S. Lind has provided an apt summary of this phenomenon.

> "We call it 'Political Correctness.' The name originated as something of a joke, literally in a comic strip, and we tend still to think of it as only half-serious. In fact, it's deadly serious. It is the great disease of our century, the disease that has left tens of millions of people dead in Europe, in Russia, in China, indeed around the world. It is the disease of ideology. PC is not funny. PC is deadly serious. If we look at it analytically, if we look at it historically, we quickly find out exactly what it is. Political Correctness is cultural Marxism. It is Marxism translated from economic into cultural terms. It is an effort that goes back not to the 1960s and the hippies and the peace movement, but back to World War I. If we compare the basic tenets of Political Correctness with classical Marxism the parallels are very obvious. First of all, both are totalitarian ideologies. The totalitarian nature of Political Correctness is revealed nowhere more clearly than on college campuses, many of which at this point are small ivy covered North Koreas, where the student or faculty member who dares to cross any of the lines set up by the gender feminist or the homosexual-rights activists, or the local black or Hispanic group, or any of the other sainted 'victims' groups that PC revolves around, quickly find themselves in judicial trouble. Within the small legal system of the college, they face formal charges – some star-chamber proceeding – and punishment."

The question of "political correctness" is one that I discovered entirely by accident. As an activist on the margins of the radical Left during the late 1980s and early 1990s, I first became exposed to the censorious, inquisitorial, and hysterical attitudes and actions that are now all too frequently common among the proponents of political correctness. At the time, I was inclined to dismiss such occurrences as mere manifestations of excessive zeal by otherwise well-intentioned persons.

1

Introduction

During the course of the subsequent decade, I came to realize that political correctness was not simply priggishness with a progressive face, but a representation of a longstanding tradition within the Left that has existed since the time of the French Revolution. The hallmark of leftist thought is its insistence upon universal human equality and the sanctity of "progress." There is a pronounced tendency among leftists to adopt a dualistic worldview that defines social and political conflict in terms of the persistent struggle between the forces of reaction and progress, with the former representing darkness and evil and the latter representing justice and virtue. Consequently, leftist movements often assume a religious character in a way that reflects the messianic or apocalyptic zeal often associated with fundamentalism. Just as the fundamentalist crusader feels the need to purge the world of sin or heresy, so does the leftist crusader experience a similar impulse to engage in a holy war against particular manifestations of perceived inequality. These may include racism, sexism, homophobia, xenophobia, classism, Islamophobia, climate change denial, transphobia, patriarchy, hierarchy, looksism, ablism, fatphobia, speciesism, or any other perceived offense against equality. Meanwhile, the list of such offenses becomes increasingly absurd and implausible.

In more recent times, it has become fashionable to refer to politically correct leftist zealots of these kinds as "social justice warriors." However, this label is a bit of a misnomer as the objectives of such people are quite anti-social and have little to do with "justice" in any recognizable sense. The essays that are included in this collection constitute an effort to explain actually what political correctness is, from where it originated, and the ominous nature of its implications. It is argued in these writings that political correctness is simply a manifestation of the tendency towards political totalitarianism of the kind that plagued the twentieth century. Political correctness is a representation of an identifiable ideological outlook that regards any limits on the pursuit of power in the name of equality and progress to be intolerable. This is clearly demonstrated by the contempt that is often shown by proponents of political correctness for the autonomy of civil society, the separation of powers, standards of due process, and the conventional liberties of speech, religion, association, property, or privacy.

I approach these questions from the perspective of a philosophical anarchist who maintains three primary concerns regarding the dangers that are posed by political correctness. First, as an anarchist,

The Tyranny of the Politically Correct

I am profoundly critical of the degree to which so many in the general anarchist milieu have adopted and internalized the ideological values and behavioral norms associated with political correctness. I consider this to be the greatest failure and most damaging weakness of contemporary anarchist movements. Second, I regard political correctness as a divisive and destructive force that undermines efforts to build movements to address the most pressing challenges of the present era, such as the ongoing centralization of capital on an international level, the rise of the surveillance state, and the hegemony of American imperialism and its related wars of aggression. Lastly, the ideological framework of political correctness is increasingly being incorporated into the self-legitimizing ideological superstructure of the state just as a theocratic regime might incorporate an interpretation of a particular religion as its own means of self-legitimization.

While I approach these questions and concerns from the perspective of a philosophical anarchist as the content of some of the essays in this work will indicate, this collection is not intended to be read solely by anarchists. Instead, this work is intended to be a resource for all of those who are concerned about the excesses of arbitrary power, whether liberal, conservative, left or right, religious or secular, socialist or capitalist. One need not agree with every claim that is made or every conclusion that is drawn in this collection in order to recognize the inherent dangers of unrestrained power masked by moral zealotry. Just as opposition to Stalinist regimes of the twentieth century normally spanned the spectrum of political opinion from conservative traditionalists to dissident socialists, so must the opposition to political correctness become the project of all those who would stand against oppression claiming legitimacy in the name of a closed ideological system.

Keith Preston

April 21, 2016

1

The New Totalitarianism

Regular readers of the Lew Rockwell blog (www.lewrockwell.com) are no doubt familiar with the criticisms of Marxism to be found within the classical liberal, traditional conservative and modern libertarian intellectual traditions. However, I come from another tradition that contains within itself those thinkers who were among the very first to recognize what the proponents of authoritarian, statist socialism were up to. Who would the reader suppose was the author who characterized the Jacobins, Blanquists and Marxists as those who would "...reconstruct society upon an imaginary plan, much like the astronomers who for respect for their calculations would make over the system of the universe..."? Ludwig von Mises? Friedrich August von Hayek? Murray Rothbard? No, it was Pierre-Joseph Proudhon, the first thinker to ever call himself an anarchist. Who would one suspect of issuing the following critique of Marxism?

> *The expression of 'learned socialist', 'scientific socialism'...which continually appear in the speeches and writings of the followers of ...Marx, prove that the pseudo-People's State will be nothing but a despotic control of the population by a new and not at all numerous aristocracy of real and pseudo scientists. The 'uneducated' people will be totally relieved of the cares of administration and will be treated as a regimented herd. A beautiful liberation indeed!*

This prediction of the logical outcome of state-run economies predates the "new class" theory pioneered by the likes of Max Nomad, George Orwell and James Burnham by nearly a century. Its author is the renegade Russian aristocrat and number-one rival of Karl Marx, the classical anarchist godfather Mikhail Bakunin. And nearly one hundred fifty years before the venerable Professor Hans Hermann Hoppe published his thoroughly radical and compelling critique of the modern deification of "democracy," Proudhon said of the mindset similar to that exhibited by those whom Lew Rockwell has characterized as "red state fascists":

> "...because of this ignorance of the primitiveness of their instincts, of the urgency of their needs, of the impatience of their desires, the

people show a preference toward summary forms of authority. The thing they are looking for is not legal guarantees, of which they do not have any idea and whose power they do not understand, they do not care for intricate mechanisms or for checks and balances for which, on their own account, they have no use, it is a boss in whose word they confide, a leader whose intentions are known to the people and who devotes himself to its interests, that they are seeking. This chief they provided with limitless authority and irresistible power. Inclined toward suspicion and calumny, but incapable of methodical discussion, they believe in nothing definite save the human will.

Left to themselves or led by their tribunes the masses never established anything. They have their face turned backwards; no tradition is formed among them; no orderly spirit, no idea which acquires the force of law. Of politics they understand nothing except the element of intrigue; of the art of governing, nothing except prodigality and force; of justice nothing but mere indictment; of liberty, nothing but the ability to set up idols which are smashed the next morning. The advent of democracy starts an era of retrogression which will ensure the death of the nation...

Having been an adherent of the classical anarchist outlook for nearly two decades and a participant, whether directly or peripherally, in the culture of the radical Left during that time, my own political background has given me some important insights into what is going on politically in our country and in Western civilization today.

Historically, classical liberals, libertarians, traditionalist conservatives, classical anarchists and, quite frequently, religious believers and even dissident socialists have fervently resisted the onslaught of the greatest evil of modernity, that of the totalitarian state. Though I am a traditional Bakuninist anarchist and most of those reading this are likely in the libertarian, paleoconservative, classical liberal or anarcho-capitalist camps, most of us would no doubt agree that the state and the concentrated power it represents is among the gravest threats to human life, liberty, culture and civilization. Therefore, we have reason to value one another. Most of us are instinctively inclined to associate the totalitarian state with the ideology of Marxism. Given that the concept of state-directed "command" economies has fallen into intellectual disrepute in recent decades, some are inclined to regard Marxism as having been relegated to the garbage heap of once prevalent but now discarded intellectual frameworks in the same manner as Zeus worship or the Ptolemaic model of the universe. Nothing could be further from the truth.

Orthodox Marxists, particularly Stalinists, were in their heyday fond of referring to heretics within their own ranks as "revisionists." Enver Hoxha's polemics against the "de-Stalinized" Communist parties of Western Europe in the 1960s and 1970s come to mind. Yet, the branch of Marxist "revisionism" that should be of the most concern to us today is that whose roots can be traced to the Frankfurt School of the 1930s and its subsequent influence on the so-called "New Left" of the 1960s. Fortunately, LRC's own regular contributor William Lind has elsewhere summarized the foundations of this system of thought, thereby saving me the trouble of having to do so. Says Mr. Lind:

> What the Frankfurt School essentially does is draw on both Marx and Freud in the 1930s to create this theory called Critical Theory. The term is ingenious because you're tempted to ask, "What is the theory?" The theory is to criticize. The theory is that the way to bring down Western culture and the capitalist order is not to lay down an alternative. They explicitly refuse to do that. They say it can't be done, that we can't imagine what a free society would look like (their definition of a free society). As long as we're living under repression – the repression of a capitalistic economic order which creates (in their theory) the Freudian condition, the conditions that Freud describes in individuals of repression – we can't even imagine it. What Critical Theory is about is simply criticizing. It calls for the most destructive criticism possible, in every possible way, designed to bring the current order down. And, of course, when we hear from the feminists that the whole of society is just out to get women and so on, that kind of criticism is a derivative of Critical Theory. It is all coming from the 1930s, not the 1960s...

> ...These origins of Political Correctness would probably not mean too much to us today except for two subsequent events. The first was the student rebellion in the mid-1960s, which was driven largely by resistance to the draft and the Vietnam War. But the student rebels needed theory of some sort. They couldn't just get out there and say, 'Hell no we won't go,' they had to have some theoretical explanation behind it. Very few of them were interested in wading through Das Kapital. Classical, economic Marxism is not light, and most of the radicals of the 60s were not deep. Fortunately for them, and unfortunately for our country today, and not just in the university, Herbert Marcuse remained in America when the Frankfurt School relocated back to Frankfurt after the war. And whereas Mr. Adorno in Germany is appalled by the student rebellion when it breaks out there – when the student rebels come into Adorno's classroom,

> *he calls the police and has them arrested – Herbert Marcuse, who*
> *remained here, saw the 60s student rebellion as the great chance. He*
> *saw the opportunity to take the work of the Frankfurt School and*
> *make it the theory of the New Left in the United States."*

When I first read the transcript of Mr. Lind's lecture, I was reminded of the following passage from the autobiography of 1960s counterculture icon Abbie Hoffman, describing the scene at a speech given by Herbert Marcuse during the late 1960s:

> *Marcuse was, with the exception of Maslow, the teacher who had*
> *the greatest impact on me. I studied with him at Brandeis, and later*
> *attended his lectures at the University of California. In the spring*
> *of '67, I saw him speaking-of all places-at the Fillmore East. There*
> *he was, this statuesque, white-haired seventy-year old European*
> *Marxist scholar, following the Group Image acid-rock band onto*
> *the stage, accompanied by the thunderous foot-stomping cheers*
> *of America's most stoned-out, anti-intellectual generation....Ben*
> *Motherfucker, leader of the Lower East Side's most nefarious street*
> *gang, spat on the floor, raised his fist, and exclaimed, "Dat cat's duh*
> *only fuckin' brain worth listnin' to in de cuntree!*

Of course, this eerie scene resembles nothing quite so much as a sixties counterculture version of the Nuremberg Rallies. The reader may be wondering what such an obscure bit of American folk history has to do with contemporary world politics. To understand the significance of what I have described here, we need to examine some further developments in American political history.

The Sixty-Eighters and Totalitarian Humanism

The radicals of the 1960s were first and foremost proponents of a cultural revolution. Though theirs might not have been quite so brutal as the "cultural revolution" going on in China at the same time, it was a cultural revolution nevertheless. During the First Gulf War of 1990–91, I became involved with what passed for an antiwar movement at the time and I once put the question to a then–middle-aged veteran of the antiwar Left of the sixties, a former member of the Students for a Democratic Society, of what he thought his generation had actually achieved, given that the US empire and its imperialist wars seemed to still be going strong. He reflected on the question for a moment and then replied that the problem with sixties radicalism was that it was a cultural movement, primarily involved with questions of race, gender, ecology, sexuality and the like, and had achieved great victories in those areas, but had achieved virtually nothing in the realms of politics, economics or foreign policy. Therefore, the US empire that emerged during the early Cold War period remained intact and largely unscathed, in spite of the upheavals of the 1960s.

That is exactly right. The cultural left of the sixties has since gone on to become largely the status quo. Many people no doubt wonder whatever happened to the hippies, the student radicals, the antiwar protestors of that time. Where are they today? Shouldn't they be more visible given the similarities of that time to the present time? Dr. Tomislav Sunic provides a partial answer with this description of what has since transpired:

> Back then, the 68ers had cultural power in their hands, controlling the best universities and spreading their permissive sensibility. Students were obliged to bow down to the unholy trinity of Marx, Freud, and Sartre, and the humanities curriculum showed the first signs of anti-Europeanism. Today, the 68ers (or 'neo-liberals' or social democrats) have grown up, and they have changed not only their name, but also their habitat and their discourse. Their time has come: Now they hold both cultural and political power. From Buenos Aires to Quai d'Orsay, from 1600 Pennsylvania Avenue to 10 Downing Street, they sit in air-conditioned executive offices or in ministerial cabinets, and they behave as if nothing has changed. Perfectly recycled in stylish Gucci suits, wearing expensive Bally shoes, sporting fine mascara, the 68ers pontificate about the global free market. They have embraced their former foe, capitalist entrepreneurship, and have added to it the fake humanistic facade of socialist philanthropy...

> They have drawn up a hit list, filled with the names of senile individuals from distant countries who have been accused of 'war crimes' and must be extradited to the 68ers' kangaroo courts. Seldom, if ever, do they acknowledge the millions of victims of communism, documented recently by Stephane Courtois in Le livre noire du communisme. Nor do they wish to face their own role in communist genocide. And why should they? Their decades-long civil disobedience resulted in the downplaying of communist horror and legitimized the Gulag. While the 68ers did not play a direct role in Beria's, Yagoda's, or Tito's ethnic cleansing, they were useful idiots. If today's caviar left were to open the Pandora's box of the Gulag, Augusto Pinochet would look like a naughty little scout from boot

camp. The best way to cover up their own murderous past is to sing the hymns of human rights and to lecture on the metaphysics of permanent economic progress...

The 68ers and their well-clad cronies are the financial insiders now, speculating on stocks, never hesitating to transfer megabucks to Luxembourg via the Cayman Islands or, better yet, to do some hidden wheeling and dealing on Wall Street. They no longer spout nonsense about equality and social justice for the Vietcong, Congolese, or Tibetans, nor do they indulge in academic rantings about a socialist utopia. And why should they? Today, the time is ripe for their gross corruption, veiled, of course, in the incessant rhetoric of multiculturalism. The 68ers have won: The world belongs to them.

The political power held today by the former 68ers is being institutionalized through legal restrictions on freedom of speech, of thought, and of research. Germany, Belgium, France, and other European countries have already passed strict laws forbidding young scholars to pursue open and honest research in certain touchy areas of modem history. Passages from the German Criminal Code bring to mind the Soviet comrade Vishinsky: They are not what we expect of a free and democratic country.

By quoting these passages, what I am trying to do is illustrate my core argument. Simply put, what I am really saying is that now that the radicals of the sixties have gotten older, greyer and wealthier, they have gone on to form a new kind of cultural and intellectual establishment, largely by securing their own dominance within the worlds of academia, media and entertainment. Further, the end result of this dominance has been that this new Cultural Left Establishment has formed an alliance with the older, pre-existing political, economic and military establishment. What the proponents of the sixties cultural revolution have, in essence, done is rather than overthrow the US empire, they have seized control of that empire and are using it for their own purposes, which may or may not overlap with the interests of the older establishment. The creeping totalitarianism we see evolving today is an outgrowth of Marxism, not necessarily in the orthodox socialist sense, but in the re-application of Marxist theory to cultural matters, where the 'official victims' of Western civilization replace the proletariat as the focus of a dualistic struggle for political power. The emerging ideology of the Western, particularly American, ruling classes can, I believe, be described as follows:

Militarism, Imperialism and Empire in the guise of 'human rights', 'democracy', modernity, universalism, feminism and other leftist shibboleths.

Corporate Mercantilism (or 'state-capitalism') under the guise of 'free trade'.

In domestic policy, what I call 'totalitarian humanism' whereby an all-encompassing and unaccountable bureaucracy peers into every corner of society to make sure no one anywhere, anyplace, anytime ever practices 'racism, sexism, homophobia', smoking, 'sex abuse' or other such leftist sins.

In the realm of law, a police state ostensibly designed to protect everyone from terrorism, crime, drugs, guns, gangs or some other bogeyman of the month.

The kind of state that proponents of this new ideology envision is one where the purpose of local government is to enforce leftist orthodoxy against competing institutions (like families, religions, businesses, unions, clubs, other associations), the purpose of national government is to enforce leftism against local communities, and the purpose of foreign policy is to enforce leftism against "backward" or "reactionary" traditional societies.

It should also be pointed out that the old-guard Marxists, even the Stalinists, only took their egalitarianism so far. Their professed aims were limited to the ostensible equality of wealth among the social classes and, in some instances, political equality of racial and ethnic groups. They did not nearly go so far as to attack the long list of "isms," "archies" and "phobias" (for instance, "looksism," "phallocracy''" or "transphobia") so reviled by today's leftoids, nor did they typically advocate equality of looks, weight, ability, intelligence or even species (hence, the modern leftist infatuation with concepts ranging from "grade inflation" to virtual prohibition of so-called "fatty foods" to giving animals legal rights approximating those of humans). Nor did they advocate ending race and gender oppression by simply abolishing races and genders. Indeed, the contemporary leftist obsession with both race and health under the banner of multiculturalism and the therapeutic state calls to mind the other great totalitarian ideology of the twentieth century. One shudders to think what will happen when these elements gain control of a more fully developed genetic engineering technology and subsequently combine this with emerging surveillance technologies. An increasingly popular concept in leftist academic circles is the notion of "whiteness" which, as might be expected, is typically used as a term of opprobrium. Indeed, one of the more extreme proponents of "whiteness" theory maintains a website whose masthead reads "treason to whiteness is loyalty to humanity." To understand the implications of this slogan, one need only remove the term "whiteness" and replace it with "Jewishness."

2

The Ideology of Totalitarian Humanism

Many on the alternative Right are inclined to refer to PC as "cultural Marxism." In some ways, this is an apt metaphor, as the PC ideology bears a resemblance to the reductionist concept of class antagonism that orthodox Marxism advances. If the dualistic class dichotomy of "proletarians and bourgeoisie" is replaced with a newer dichotomy pitting feminist women, minorities, gays, immigrants, the transgendered and others having been or believed to be oppressed against the "hegemony" of "straight, white, Christian, males," then similarities between PC and Marxism do indeed emerge. However, PC could in some ways be compared with totalitarianism from the other end of the political spectrum. If the duality of "Aryans" believed to be oppressed by and in mortal struggle with "the Jews" is replaced with the aforementioned dichotomy advanced by PC, a reductionism of comparable crudity likewise becomes apparent. Yet it would seem to me that such metaphors as "cultural Marxism" or "liberal Nazism" are not really the best characterizations of PC.

The best label for PC I ever encountered was "totalitarian humanism." I can't take credit for this term. I lifted it from an anonymous underground writer some years ago. Read the original essay here. Here's a particularly enlightened part:

When one looks up the word 'Humanism' in an encyclopedia it states that Humanism is an ideology which focuses on the importance of every single human being. That it is an "ideology which emphasizes the value of the individual human being and its ability to develop into a harmonic and culturally aware personality". This sounds fair enough, right? Indeed it does, but it is my firm belief that the explanation here does not match the humanism of our time.

The so-called Humanists I have met have been putting a strong emphasis on humanity as a gigantic community rather than on the individual. Often one will even find alleged humanists who insist that the views, aspirations and basic happiness of indigenous Europeans is of no importance. Instead, these Humanists say, indigenous Europeans should bow down and forget about their own wants and desires for the greater good of humanity. The greater good of Humanity usually seems to take no interest in Europe's cultural heritage and it's integration into a grey, world-wide, uniform "globalization" with the Coca-Cola culture as loadstar.

Totalitarian humanism is a derivative of the classical Jacobin ideology that loves an abstract and universal "humanity" so much that its proponents don't care what has to be done to individual human beings or particular human cultures in order to advance their ideals. Perhaps the best summary of the political outlook of totalitarian humanism was provided by the maverick psychiatrist and critic of the "therapeutic state," Thomas Szasz:

> *In the nineteenth century, a liberal was a person who championed individual liberty in a context of laissez-faire economics, who defined liberty as the absence of coercion, and who regarded the state as an ever-present threat to personal freedom and responsibility. Today, a liberal is a person who champions social justice in a context of socialist economics, who defines liberty as access to the means for a good life, and who regards the state as a benevolent provider whose duty is to protect people from poverty, racism, sexism, illness, and drugs.*

Dr. Szasz wrote that passage nearly twenty years ago. Nowadays, the laundry list of "poverty, racism, sexism, illness, and drugs" might be lengthened to include classism, ageism, homophobia, xenophobia, ableism, lookism, fatphobia, thinism, beautyism, transphobia, producerism, "appearance discrimination," speciesism, adultcentrism, pedophobia, chronocentrism, and other creative efforts at dictionary expansion. Likewise, the therapeutic component of totalitarian humanism has expanded so as to include the supposed necessity of state action to save us all from fatty foods, salt, smoking, and soda vending machines in public schools. Like all totalitarian ideologies, totalitarian humanism has its contradictions, hypocrisies, and absurdities. For instance, public acts of anal intercourse are regarded as virtuous and courageous manifestations of human liberation and personal fulfillment, while smoking in bars or even in strip clubs is a grave menace to public health. Suggestive music videos and violent video games are symptomatic of an oppressively patriarchal and testosterone-fueled society, while surgically altering one's "gender identity" is just routine day-to-day business, like getting a tattoo.

The Tyranny of the Politically Correct

As one with something of a taste for the bizarre and eccentric, I might find the PC circus to be little more than a philistine but amusing bit of outrageous entertainment, akin to professional wrestling or the old freak shows of carnivals past, if it weren't for the fact that these folks are hell-bent on imposing their "ideals" on the rest of us by force of the state. Totalitarian humanism is a war on sovereignty. It is a war on the sovereignty of individuals against arbitrary and coercive authority, the sovereignty of non-state institutions against political authority, the sovereignty of organic communities against a centralized leviathan, the sovereignty of nations against global entities, the sovereignty of history, tradition, and culture against prescriptive and prohibitive ideology. Totalitarian humanism is an effort to reduce all of us to the level of dependent serfs on a plantation ruled by an army of overly zealous concerned mommies and busy-body social workers backed up by the S.W.A.T. team and paramilitary police. Give me beautyism or give me death.

3

Herbert Marcuse and the
Tolerance of Repression

"I am not bound to defend liberal notions of tolerance."
– Left-wing anarchist activist to the author.

The rise of the New Left is typically considered to have its origins in the student rebellions of the late 1960s and early 1970s when the war in Vietnam was at its height and cultural transformation was taking place in Western countries with dizzying rapidity. Yet scholars have long recognized that the intellectual roots of the New Left were created several decades earlier through the efforts of the thinkers associated with the Institute for Social Research (commonly known as the "Frankfurt School") to reconsider the essence of Marxist theory following the failure of the working classes of Western Europe to produce a socialist revolution as orthodox Marxism had predicted.

The support shown for their respective national states by the European working classes, and indeed by the Socialist parties of Europe themselves, during the Great War which had broken out in 1914 had generated a crisis of faith for Marxist theoreticians. Marx had taught that the working classes had no country of their own and that the natural loyalties of the workers were not to their nations but to their socioeconomic class and its material interests. Marxism predicted a class revolution that would transcend national and cultural boundaries and regarded such concepts as national identity and cultural traditions as nothing more than hollow concepts generated by the broader ideological superstructure of capitalism (and feudalism before it) that served to legitimize the established mode of production. Yet the patriotic fervor shown by the workers during the war, the failure of the workers to carry out a class revolution even after the collapse of capitalism during the interwar era, and the rise of fascism during the same period all indicated that something was amiss concerning Marxist orthodoxy. The thinkers of the Frankfurt School sought to reconsider Marxism in light of these events without jettisoning the core precepts of Marxism, such as its critique of the political economy of capitalism, alienation, and the material basis of ideological hegemony.

The Institute attracted many genuine and interesting scholars some of whom were luminaries of the unique and fascinating German intellectual culture of the era of the Weimar Republic. Among these were Max Horkheimer, Theodor Adorno, Otto Kirchheimer, Franz Neumann, and Erich Fromm. But the thinker associated with the Institute who would ultimately have the greatest influence was the philosopher and political theorist Herbert Marcuse (1898-1979). The reach of Marcuse's influence is indicated by the fact that during the student uprisings in France during 1968, which very nearly toppled the regime of Charles De Gaulle, graffiti would appear on public buildings with the slogan: "Marx, Mao, Marcuse." Arguably, there was no intellectual who had a greater impact on the development of the New Left than Marcuse.

When the Nazis came to power in 1933, Marcuse and other members of the Frankfurt School immigrated to the United States and reestablished the Institute at Columbia University in New York City. Marcuse became a United States citizen in 1940 and during World War Two was employed by the Office of War Information, Office of Strategic Services (the forerunner to the Central Intelligence Agency), and the U.S. Department of State. Throughout the 1950s and 1960s, Marcuse was a professor of political theory at Columbia, Harvard, Brandeis, and the University of California at San Diego. During his time in academia, Marcuse continued the efforts to revise Marxism in light of the conditions of an industrially advanced mid-twentieth century society. One of his most influential works was an effort to synthesize Marx and Freud, Eros and Civilization, published in 1955, and One Dimensional Man, a critique of the consumer culture of the postwar era and the integration of the traditional working classes into the consumer culture generated by capitalism. Both of these works became major texts for the student activists of the New Left.

Because of his legacy as an intellectual godfather of the New Left and the radical social movements of the 1960s and 1970s generally, Marcuse is not surprisingly a rather polarizing figure in contemporary intellectual discourse regarding those fields where his thinking has gained tremendous influence. Much of the curriculum of the humanities departments in Western universities is essentially derived from the thought of Marcuse and his contemporaries, particularly in sociology, anthropology, gender studies, ethnic studies, and studies of sexuality, but also in history, psychology, and literature. It is quite certain that if Marcuse and his fellow scholars from the Frankfurt School, such as Adorno and Horkheimer, were still alive today they would no doubt be regarded as god-like figures by contemporary leftist academics and students. From the other end of the political spectrum, many partisans of the political right, traditionalists, religious fundamentalists, nationalists, and social conservatives regard Marcuse as the personification of evil. Because the legacy of Marcuse's work is so controversial and polarizing, it is important to develop a rational understanding of what his most influential ideas actually were.

Although he remained a Marxist until his death, Marcuse was never an apologist for the totalitarian regimes that had emerged in Communist countries. Indeed, he wrote in defense of dissidents who were subject to repression under those regimes, such as the East German dissident Rudolf Bahro. Marcuse considered orthodox Marxism as lacking concern for the individual and criticized what he regarded as the insufficiently libertarian character of Marxism. Like many associated with the New Left, he often expressed a preference for the writings of the younger Marx, which have a humanistic orientation inspired by the idealism of nineteenth century utopian socialism, as opposed to the turgid and ideologically rigid writings of the elder Marx. The thinkers of the Frankfurt School had also been influenced by the Weberian critique of the massive growth of bureaucracy in modern societies and strongly criticized the hyper-bureaucratic tendencies of both capitalist and communist countries as they were during the Cold War period.

Marcuse regarded the consumer culture that emerged during the postwar economic boom as representing a form of social control produced and maintained by capitalism. According to Marcuse, capitalist productivity had grown to the level where the industrial proletariat was no longer the impoverished wage slaves of Marx's era. Economic growth, technological expansion, and the successes of labor reform movements in Western countries, had allowed the working classes to achieve a middle class standard of living and become integrated into the wider institutional framework of capitalism. Consequently, workers in advanced industrial societies no longer held any revolutionary potential and had become loyal subjects of the state in the same manner as the historic bourgeoisie before them. This by itself is not an original or even particularly insightful observation. However, Marcuse did not believe that the rising living standards and institutional integration of the working classes represented an absence of exploitation. Rather, Marcuse felt that the consumer culture made available by affluent industrial societies had multiple deleterious effects.

First, consumer culture had the effect of "buying off" the workers by offering them a lifestyle of relative comfort and material goods in exchange for their continuing loyalty to capitalism and indifference to struggles for social and political change. Second, consumer culture created a kind of a false consciousness among the public at large through the use of the advertising industry and mass media generally to inculcate the values of consumerism and to essentially create unnecessary wants and perceived needs among the population. The effect of this is that people were working more than they really needed to sustain themselves in order to achieve the values associated with consumer culture. This created not only the psychological damaging "rat race" lifestyle of the competitive capitalist workforce and marketplace, but generated excessive waste (demonstrated by such phenomena as "planned obsolescence," for example), environmental destruction, and even imperialist war for the conquest of newer capitalist markets, access to material resources, and the thwarting of movements for self-determination or social change in underdeveloped parts of the world. Third, Marcuse saw a relationship between the domination of consumer culture and the outlandishly repressive sexual mores of the 1950s era (where the term "pregnant" was banned from American television, for instance). According to Marcuse, the consumerist ethos generated by capitalism expected the individual to experience pleasure through material acquisition and consumption rather than through sexual expression or participation. The worker was expected to forgo sex in favor of work and channel libidinal drives into consumerist drives. Material consumption was the worker's reward for avoiding erotic pleasure. For this reason, Marcuse regarded sexual expression and participation (what he famously called "polymorphous perversity") as a potential force for the subversion of the capitalist system. As the sexual revolution grew in the 1960s, student radicals would champion this view with the slogan "make love, not war."

As the working class had ceased to be a revolutionary force, Marcuse began to look to other social groups as potentially viable catalysts for radical social and political change. These included the array of the traditionally subordinated, excluded, or marginalized such as racial minorities, feminists, homosexuals, and young people, along with privileged and educated critics of the status quo such as radical intellectuals. Marcuse personally outlined and developed much of the intellectual foundation of the radical movements of the 1960s and exerted much personal influence on leading figures in these movements. The Black Panther figure Angela Davis and the Youth International Party ("Yippie") founder and "Chicago Seven" defendant

Abbie Hoffman had both been students of Marcuse while he taught at Brandeis. However, it would be a mistake to regard Marcuse as having somehow been a leader or founder of these movements. Marcuse did not so much serve as a radical leader during the upheavals of the 1960s and 1970s as much as he was an interpreter of social and political currents that were then emerging and a scholar who provided ideas with which discontented thinkers and activists could identify. It is often argued by some on the political right that the thinkers of the Frankfurt School hatched a nefarious plot to destroy Western civilization through the seizure and subversion of cultural institutions. This theory suggests that radical Marxists came to believe that they must first control institutions that disseminate ideas such as education and entertainment in order to remove the false consciousness previously inculcated in the masses by capitalist domination over these institutions before the masses can achieve the level of radical consciousness necessary to carry out a socialist revolution. Those on the right with an inclination towards anti-Semitism will also point out that most of the luminaries of the Frankfurt School, such as Marcuse, were ethnic Jews.

Yet the cultural revolution of the 1960s and 1970s was the product of a convergence of a vast array of forces. The feminist revolution, for instance, had as much to do with the integration of women into the industrial workforce during World War Two while the men were absent fighting the war and the need for an ever greater pool of skilled workers in an expanding industrial economy during a time of tremendous technological advancement and population growth as it does with the ambitions of far left radicals. The real fuel behind the growth of the youth and student movements of the 1960s was the war in Vietnam and the desire of many young people of conscription age to avoid death and dismemberment in a foolish war in which they had no stake. The sexual revolution was made possible in large part by the invention of the birth control pill and the mass production of penicillin which reduced the health and social risks associated with sexual activity. The racial revolution of the era was rooted in centuries old conflicts and struggles that had been given new impetus by growing awareness of the excesses which occurred during the Nazi period. The heightened interest in environmental conservation, concerns for populations with serious disadvantages (such as the disabled or mentally ill), increased emphasis on personal fulfillment and physical and psychological health, and concern for social and political rights beyond those of a purely material nature all reflect the achievements and ambitions of an affluent, post-scarcity society where basic material needs are largely met. Suffice to say that the transformation of an entire civilization in the space of a decade can hardly be attributed to the machinations of a handful of European radicals forty years earlier.

There is actually much of value in the work of the Frankfurt School scholars. They are to be commended for their honest confrontation with some of the failings and weaknesses of Marxist orthodoxy even while many of their fellow Marxists continued to cling uncritically to an outmoded doctrine. Marcuse and his colleagues are to be respected for their skepticism regarding the authoritarian communist states when many of their contemporaries, such as Jean Paul Sartre, embraced regimes of this type with appalling naiveté. The critique of consumer culture and the "culture industry" offered by Marcuse, Horkheimer, and others may itself be one-dimensional and lacking in nuance at times, but it does raise valid and penetrating questions about a society that has become so relentlessly media-driven and oriented towards fads and fashions in such a "bread and circuses" manner. However, while Marcuse was neither a god nor a devil, but merely a scholar and thinker whose ideas were both somewhat prescient and reflective of the currents of his time, there is an aspect to his thought that has left a genuinely pernicious influence. In 1965, Marcuse published an essay titled, "Repressive Tolerance," which foreshadows very clearly the direction in which left-wing opinion and practice has developed since that time.

The essay is essentially an argument against the Western liberal tradition rooted in the thinking of Locke, with its Socratic and Scholastic precedents, which came into political reality in the nineteenth century and which was a monumental achievement for civilization. In this essay, Marcuse regurgitates the conventional Marxist line that freedom of opinion and speech in a liberal state is a bourgeois sham that only masks capitalist hegemony and domination. Of course, there is some truth to this claim. As Marcuse said:

> But with the concentration of economic and political power and the integration of opposites in a society which uses technology as an instrument of domination, effective dissent is blocked where it could freely emerge; in the formation of opinion, in information and communication, in speech and assembly. Under the rule of monopolistic media – themselves the mere instruments of economic and political power – a mentality is created for which right and wrong, true and false are predefined wherever they affect the vital interests of the society. This is, prior to all expression and communication,

a matter of semantics: the blocking of effective dissent, of the recognition of that which is not of the Establishment which begins in the language that is publicized and administered. The meaning of words is rigidly stabilized. Rational persuasion, persuasion to the opposite is all but precluded.

Marcuse proceeds from this observation not to advocate for institutional or economic structures that might make the practical and material means of communication or expression more readily available to more varied or dissenting points of view but to attack liberal conceptions of tolerance altogether.

These background limitations of tolerance are normally prior to the explicit and judicial limitations as defined by the courts, custom, governments, etc. (for example, "clear and present danger", threat to national security, heresy). Within the framework of such a social structure, tolerance can be safely practiced and proclaimed. It is of two kinds: (1) the passive toleration of entrenched and established attitudes and ideas even if their damaging effect on man and nature is evident, and (2) the active, official tolerance granted to the Right as well as to the Left, to movements of aggression as well as to movements of peace, to the party of hate as well as to that of humanity. I call this non-partisan tolerance "abstract" or "pure" inasmuch as it refrains from taking sides – but in doing so it actually protects the already established machinery of discrimination. This statement reflects the by now quite familiar leftist claim that non-leftist opinions are being offered from a position of privilege or hegemony and are therefore by definition unworthy of being heard. Marcuse argues that tolerance has a higher purpose:

The telos [goal] of tolerance is truth. It is clear from the historical record that the authentic spokesmen of tolerance had more and other truth in mind than that of propositional logic and academic theory. John Stuart Mill speaks of the truth which is persecuted in history and which does not triumph over persecution by virtue of its "inherent power", which in fact has no inherent power "against the dungeon and the stake". And he enumerates the "truths" which were cruelly and successfully liquidated in the dungeons and at the stake: that of Arnold of Brescia, of Fra Dolcino, of Savonarola, of the Albigensians, Waldensians, Lollards, and Hussites. Tolerance is first and foremost for the sake of the heretics – the historical road toward humanitas appears as heresy: target of persecution by the powers that be. Heresy by itself, however, is no token of truth.

23

This statement at face value might be beyond reproach were it not for its implicit suggestion that only leftists and those favored by leftists can ever rightly be considered among the ranks of the unjustly "persecuted" or among those who have truth to tell. Marcuse goes on to offer his own version of "tolerance" in opposition to conventional, empirical, value neutral notions of tolerance of the kind associated with the liberal tradition.

Liberating tolerance, then, would mean intolerance against movements from the Right and toleration of movements from the Left. As to the scope of this tolerance and intolerance: ... it would extend to the stage of action as well as of discussion and propaganda, of deed as well as of word. The traditional criterion of clear and present danger seems no longer adequate to a stage where the whole society is in the situation of the theater audience when somebody cries: "fire". It is a situation in which the total catastrophe could be triggered off any moment, not only by a technical error, but also by a rational miscalculation of risks, or by a rash speech of one of the leaders. In past and different circumstances, the speeches of the Fascist and Nazi leaders were the immediate prologue to the massacre. The distance between the propaganda and the action, between the organization and its release on the people had become too short. But the spreading of the word could have been stopped before it was too late: if democratic tolerance had been withdrawn when the future leaders started their campaign, mankind would have had a chance of avoiding Auschwitz and a World War.

> *The whole post-fascist period is one of clear and present danger. Consequently, true pacification requires the withdrawal of tolerance before the deed, at the stage of communication in word, print, and picture. Such extreme suspension of the right of free speech and free assembly is indeed justified only if the whole of society is in extreme danger. I maintain that our society is in such an emergency situation, and that it has become the normal state of affairs.*

Here Marcuse is clearly stating that he is not simply advocating "intolerance" of non-leftist opinion in the sense of offering criticism, rebuttal, counterargument, or even shaming, shunning, or ostracism. What he is calling for is the full fledged state repression of non-leftist opinion or expression. Nor is this repression to be limited to right-wing movements with an explicitly authoritarian agenda that aims to subvert the liberal society. Marcuse makes this very clear in a 1968 postscript to the original 1965 essay:

The Tyranny of the Politically Correct

Given this situation, I suggested in "Repressive Tolerance" the practice of discriminating tolerance in an inverse direction, as a means of shifting the balance between Right and Left by restraining the liberty of the Right, thus counteracting the pervasive inequality of freedom (unequal opportunity of access to the means of democratic persuasion) and strengthening the oppressed against the oppressed. Tolerance would be restricted with respect to movements of a demonstrably aggressive or destructive character (destructive of the prospects for peace, justice, and freedom for all). Such discrimination would also be applied to movements opposing the extension of social legislation to the poor, weak, disabled. As against the virulent denunciations that such a policy would do away with the sacred liberalistic principle of equality for "the other side", I maintain that there are issues where either there is no "other side" in any more than a formalistic sense, or where "the other side" is demonstrably "regressive" and impedes possible improvement of the human condition. To tolerate propaganda for inhumanity vitiates the goals not only of liberalism but of every progressive political philosophy.

If the choice were between genuine democracy and dictatorship, democracy would certainly be preferable. But democracy does not prevail. The radical critics of the existing political process are thus readily denounced as advocating an "elitism", a dictatorship of intellectuals as an alternative. What we have in fact is government, representative government by a non-intellectual minority of politicians, generals, and businessmen. The record of this "elite" is not very promising, and political prerogatives for the intelligentsia may not necessarily be worse for the society as a whole.

In this passage Marcuse is very clearly advocating totalitarian controls over political speech and expression that is the mirror image of the Stalinist states that he otherwise criticized for their excessive bureaucratization, economism, and repression of criticism from the Left. Marcuse makes it perfectly clear that not only perceived fascists and neo-nazis would be subject to repression under his model regime but so would even those who question the expansion of the welfare state (thereby contradicting Marcuse's criticism of bureaucracy). Marcuse states this elsewhere in "Repressive Tolerance."

Surely, no government can be expected to foster its own subversion, but in a democracy such a right is vested in the people (i.e. in the majority of the people). This means that the ways should not be blocked on which a subversive majority could develop, and if they are

25

> *blocked by organized repression and indoctrination, their reopening*
> *may require apparently undemocratic means. They would include*
> *the withdrawal of toleration of speech and assembly from groups*
> *and movements which promote aggressive policies, armament,*
> *chauvinism, discrimination on the grounds of race and religion, or*
> *which oppose the extension of public services, social security, medical*
> *care, etc"*

Marcuse's liberatory socialism is in fact to be a totalitarian bureaucracy where those who criticize leftist orthodoxy in apparently even the slightest way are to be subject to state repression. This is precisely the attitude that the authoritarian Left demonstrates at the present time. Such views are becoming increasingly entrenched in mainstream institutions and in the state under the guise of so-called "political correctness." Indeed, much of the mainstream "anarchist" movement reflects Marcuse's thinking perfectly. These "anarchists" ostensibly criticize statism, bureaucracy, capitalism, consumerism, imperialism, war, and repression, and advocate for all of the popular "social justice" causes of the day. "Tolerance" has ostensibly become the ultimate virtue for such people. Yet underneath this "tolerance" is a visceral and often violent hostility to those who dissent from leftist orthodoxy on any number of questions in even a peripheral or moderate way. Indeed, the prevalence of this leftist intolerance within the various anarchist milieus has become the principle obstacle to the growth of a larger and more effective anarchist movement.

A functional anarchist, libertarian, or anti-state movement must first and foremost reclaim the liberal tradition of authentic tolerance of the kind that insists that decent regard for other people and a fair hearing for contending points of view on which no one ultimately has the last word must be balanced with the promulgation of ideological principles no matter how much one believes these principles to be "true." A functional and productive anarchist movement must recognize and give a seat at the table to all of the contending schools of anarchism, including non-leftist ones, and embrace those from overlapping ideologies where there is common ground. A serious anarchist movement must address points of view offered by the opposition in an objective manner that recognizes and concedes valid issues others may raise even in the face of ideological disagreement. Lastly, a genuine anarchist movement must realize that there is no issue that is so taboo that is should be taken off the table as a fitting subject for discussion and debate. Only when anarchists embrace these values will they be worthy of the name.

4

Should Libertarianism be Cultural
Leftism Minus the State?

In recent years, an idea commonly described as thick libertarianism has emerged among some libertarians. This perspective holds that libertarianism requires a commitment to a broader set of values beyond that of mere individual liberty, or the "non-aggression principle," in order to be substantive or sustainable. The "left-libertarian" writer and philosopher Charles Johnson is arguably the most prolific and articulate proponent of "thick libertarianism." In a recently published and important article on this question, Johnson begins by asking the central questions that thick libertarians wish to address:

> To what extent should libertarians concern themselves with social commitments, practices, projects or movements that seek social outcomes beyond, or other than, the standard libertarian commitment to expanding the scope of freedom from government coercion? Clearly, a consistent and principled libertarian cannot support efforts or beliefs that are contrary to libertarian principles– such as efforts to engineer social outcomes by means of government intervention. But if coercive laws have been taken off the table, what should libertarians say about other religious, philosophical, social, or cultural commitments that pursue their ends through non-coercive means, such as targeted moral agitation, mass education, artistic or literary propaganda, charity, mutual aid, public praise, ridicule, social ostracism, targeted boycotts, social investing, slow-downs and strikes in a particular shop, general strikes, or other forms of solidarity and coordinated action? Which social movements should they oppose, which should they support, and towards which should they counsel indifference? And how do we tell the difference?[1]

A survey of the writings of the leading proponents of thick libertarianism and those with similar or overlapping views makes it rather clear that,

---

1   Charles Johnson, *Libertarianism Through Thick and Thin*, The Freeman, July/ August, 2008.

for most of these thinkers, "thick libertarianism" amounts to an effort to synthesize free-market, anarcho-individualism with a far-reaching leftist outlook on cultural questions. The following comments from Roderick Long are fairly representative of this perspective:

> *In short, I'm arguing for a combination of generic universalism with specific pluralism. That is, any anarchist society, to be viable, needs to draw its dominant economic and cultural forms from the same general set, but specific selections within that set are optional. Hence the anarchist must walk a delicate line between the Scylla of excessive pluralism and the Charybdis of excessive monism. After all, …no politico-legal framework – whether statist or anarchist – exists independently of the behavior it constrains. And as Gustav Landauer is reported to have said: The State is a condition, a certain relationship between human beings, a mode of human behavior; we destroy it by contracting other relationships, by behaving differently. Since the presence or absence of the State is determined by the way people behave, and that in turn is heavily influenced by economic and cultural structures, the notion that anarchy can be entirely neutral among such structures seems hard to defend. (Of course, anarchy will be neutral in the sense that no one will be compelled to abandon the wrong economic and cultural forms, so long as they're peaceful; getting rid of such compulsion is the whole point of anarchy. But unless better forms prevail, by peaceful means, the survival of anarchy is imperiled.) Of course we can make mistakes about which economic and cultural models do or don't fit with anarchy. But then, we can make mistakes about anything. I don't see any reason for greater epistemic caution on economic and cultural matters than on political ones. Moreover, it's not as though the only reason to combat a particular economic or cultural form is that it reinforces or is reinforced by statism. Statism isn't the only bad thing in the world, after all; call me sentimental, but I think patriarchy, racism, fundamentalism, and corporate power would be worth combating even if they had no connection whatever to statism.[2]*

These comments provide an apt summary of the essence of thick libertarianism. As Charles Johnson notes, the matter of thick libertarianism "has often arisen in the context of debates over whether or not libertarianism should be integrated into a broader commitment to some of the social concerns traditionally associated with the anti-authoritarian Left, such as feminism, anti-racism, gay

---

2   Roderick Long, Anarchy Plus, Austro-Athenian Empire, November 17, 2004.

liberation, counterculturalism, labor organizing, mutual aid, and environmentalism."[3] Presumably, for "left-libertarian" proponents of thick libertarianism such as Long and Johnson, a libertarian political and economic order is more or less a natural corollary to the values of modern cultural leftism as it has emerged in the Western countries since the 1960s.

Before I critique thick libertarian arguments of this type, I wish to begin by giving due recognition to the claims of thick libertarianism that I believe to be correct. I would concur with thick libertarians that there is more to life than politics, that there are values beyond the political, that while liberty may be the highest political value it is not the only value, and that a libertarian political order is more compatible with some intellectual systems, philosophical beliefs and cultural foundations than others.

Thick libertarians have also been important participants in the effort to challenge much conventional libertarian economic dogma. Too many modern libertarians have allowed their opposition to state-socialism and the welfare-state to cloud their thinking on economic matters and many of these libertarians have become outright apologists for the corporate plutocracy, or "Republicans who take drugs" as Bob Black referred to them.[4] Libertarians would do well to study, and perhaps even incorporate into their own ideological and strategic framework, the examples provided by the classical anarchist movement of the late nineteenth and early twentieth century of anti-statist radicals who saw class-based politics as the natural complement to their libertarianism.[5] Indeed, many of those who identify with thick libertarianism to some degree or another have been at the forefront of recent efforts to move libertarianism away from its conservative image on economic matters and back to its radical roots.[6]

On many social questions, I would share ground with thick libertarians as well. Many of the conventionally "left-wing" or *left-*

---

3   Johnson, Libertarianism, *The Freeman.*

4   Bob Black, *The Libertarian As Conservative,* Address to the Eris Society, Aspen, Colorado, August, 1984.

5   Paul Avrich, *Anarchist Voices: An Oral History of Anarchism in America,* (Princeton University Press, 1996).

6   Charles Johnson, Scratching By: How Government Creates Poverty, The Freeman, December, 2007; Roderick Long, Corporations Versus The Market; Or, Whip Conflation Now, CATO Unbound, November 10, 2008.

libertarian positions held by most proponents of thick libertarianism are also my positions. I am pro-abortion, pro-euthanasia, anti-death penalty (though not for the usual reasons), pro-drug legalization, pro-gay rights and pro-sex worker rights (in the sense of opposing persecution of these groups by the state), and pro-prison abolition. I'm also pro-homeless, pro-disabled people, and pro-mentally ill, in the sense of favoring abolition of state policies impeding the self-advancement of these groups or furthering their persecution (through such measures as loitering and vagrancy laws, zoning and other laws restricting the supply of low-income housing, involuntary civil commitment, regulations restricting the activities of shelters and relief organizations and others too numerous to mention). I am also anti-drinking age, anti-compulsory schooling, anti-censorship and I would put more strident limits on the powers of the police than the ACLU would. I am also interested in anarcho-syndicalist, mutualist, distributist or "libertarian socialist" economics. These positions are well to the left of the Democratic Party, far more left than most liberals and even many hard leftists.

In terms of offering positive alternatives to the welfare state, I am very much for the development of non-state charities, relief agencies, orphanages, youth hostels, squats, shelters for battered women, the homeless or the mentally ill, self-improvement programs for drug addicts and alcoholics, assistance services for the disabled or the elderly, wildlife and environmental preserves, means of food and drug testing independent of the state bureaucracy, home schools, neighborhood schools, private schools, tenants organizations, mutual banks, credit unions, consumers unions, anarcho-syndicalist labor unions and other worker organizations, cooperatives, communes, collectives, kibbutzim and other alternative models of organizing production. I am in favor of free clinics, alternative medicine, self-diagnostic services, midwifery, the abolition of medical licensure, the repeal of prescription laws and anything else that could potentially reduce the cost of health care for the average person and diminish dependency on the medical-industrial complex and the *white coat priesthood*. Indeed, I would argue that the eventual success of libertarianism depends to a large degree on the ability of libertarians to develop workable alternatives to both the corporation-dominated economy and the state-dominated welfare and social service system. To the degree that libertarians fail to do so will be the degree to which we continue to be regarded as plutocratic apologists without concern for the unfortunate or downtrodden on the *right end*[7] or as just another species of Chomskyite *anarcho-social democrats* on the *left end.*[8]

I mention all of this for the sake of firmly establishing that I am neither an economic conservative nor a conventional *cultural conservative* of the kind found in some conservative-libertarian or paleolibertarian circles.[9] I suspect that at this point in the discussion thick libertarians and I would still be on the same page. However, where a potential problem arises involves the possible implications of statement such as this one from Johnson that I have previously referred to:

> *Recently, this question has often arisen in the context of debates over whether or not libertarianism should be integrated into a broader commitment to some of the social concerns traditionally associated with anti-authoritarian Left, such as feminism, anti-racism, gay liberation, counterculturalism, labor organizing, mutual aid, and environmentalism. Chris Sciabarra has called for a dialectical libertarianism which recognizes that Just as relations of power operate through ethical, psychological, cultural, political, and economic dimensions, so too the struggle for freedom and individualism depends upon a certain constellation of moral, psychological, and cultural factors, and in which the struggle for liberty is integrated into a comprehensive struggle for human liberation, incorporating (among other things) a commitment to gay liberation and opposition to racism.*[10]

Implicit in this statement is the view that libertarians should simply align themselves with the conventional Left on social and cultural matters, essentially taking the position of *me-tooing* the Left on most issues with the qualification of *oh, and by the way, we're also against*

7   Keith Preston, Free Enterprise: The Antidote to Corporate Plutocracy, (Libertarian Alliance, 2008).

8   Keith Preston, Anarchism or Anarcho-Social Democracy, (American Revolutionary Vanguard, 2001).

9   Keith Preston, Conservatism Is Not Enough: Reclaiming the Legacy of the Anti-State Left, (American Revolutionary Vanguard, 2001). Archived at http://attackthesystem.com/conservatism-is-not-enough-reclaiming-the-legacy-of-the-anti-state-left/; Why I Am Not a Cultural Conservative, (American Revolutionary Vanguard, 2002).

10   Johnson, Libertarianism, *The Freeman*; Chris Matthew Sciabarra, Total Freedom: Towards a Dialectical Libertarianism, (Pennsylvania State University Press, 2000).

the state, and prefer voluntary charity over government welfare. If this approach is to be followed, then libertarians will end up positioning themselves as just another branch of the radical Left right alongside Stalinists, Maoists, Trotskyites, Greens, social democrats, welfare-liberals, Marxists, anarcho-communists and the left-wing of the Democratic Party.

Libertarians would do well to learn from the lessons to be drawn from past instances where libertarians have come to regard one or another faction of the Left or Right as kindred spirits only to be eventually stabbed in the back. It has been mentioned how libertarian opponents of the welfare state have frequently been co-opted by the apologists for plutocratic conservatism. Indeed, past efforts to ally libertarianism with traditionalist conservatism have proven to be a disaster. One need only take a look at the results of William F. Buckley's New Right or Frank Meyer's *fusionism* from the 1950s and 1960s.[11] Within the context of so-called *movement conservatism,* we have the edifying spectacle of libertarians, proponents of limited government and free-market economists acting as dupes and shills for the military-industrial-complex, the right-wing of the corporate ruling class and the American empire, only to see their movement taken over eventually by the warmed-over Cold War liberals and right-wing Trotskyites that fill the ranks of the neoconservatives.[12] Not exactly a model of success, to say the least. From the other end of the political spectrum there is the experience of traditional anarchists at the hands of the Marxists since the time of the First International, including their repression by the Bolsheviks following the Russian Revolution and the treachery they encountered from the Communists during the Spanish Civil War.[13]

A similar analysis could be made regarding the relationship between

---

11   Murray N. Rothbard, Buckley Revealed, The Commonweal, January 25, 1952; Frank S. Meyer: The Fusionist as Libertarian Manque, Modern Age, 1981.

12   Justin Raimondo, Reclaiming the American Right: The Lost Legacy of the Conservative Movement, Second Edition (Intercollegiate Studies Institute, 2008).

13   Alexander Berkman, The Kronstadt Rebellion. Archived at http://dwardmac. pitzer.edu/anarchist_archives/bright/berkman/kronstadt/berkkron.html; Mikhail Bakunin, Marxism, Freedom and the State. Archived at http:// dwardmac.pitzer.edu/anarchist_archives/bakunin/marxnfree.html; Murray Bookchin, *The Spanish Anarchists: The Heroic Years 1868-1936*, (AK Press, 2001); Murray Bookchin, To Remember Spain: The Anarchist and Syndicalist Revolution of 1936, After Fifty Years: The Spanish Civil War. Archived at http:// www.spunk.org/texts/writers/bookchin/sp001642/fifty.html

libertarians and the cultural Left. Most contemporary libertarians are to some degree an outgrowth of 1960s era political and social radicalism. Libertarianism, whether in its *right* or *left* variations, really did not begin to coalesce as an organized movement until that time. [14] Previous libertarian movements had either died out or stagnated to the point of severe inertia. For this and other reasons, it should not be surprising that many libertarians continue to identify strongly with the values of sixties radicalism, including anti-racism, feminism, *gay rights,* environmentalism, counterculturalism and multiculturalism. This may be fine by itself. For instance, some libertarians may believe that anti-racism, feminism or gay liberation, among other things, are important values unto themselves, irrespective of wider politico-economic questions, just as other libertarians may believe that religious devotion, maintaining the cohesiveness of the family unit, or preserving the ethno-genetic lineage of Caucasian people (or some other people) are values of immense importance, and still other libertarians may be more concerned with the advancement of medical research, the preservation of historic architecture, bird watching, stamp collecting, soccer or rap music. So be it. I have already conceded that there may be other values of importance besides political libertarianism per se, and that such values could have meaning in their own right, irrespective of their relationship to libertarianism.

But what does any of this have to do with the struggle against the state? It should go without saying that any sort of political libertarianism worthy of the name should identify the state and its emanations such as state-privileged elites, central banking, corporatism, imperialism, militarism, police powers, penal institutions and the apparatus of statist propaganda (e.g. state-licensed media and state-run or financed education) as the primary political enemy. As a natural extension of this principle, it should likewise be recognized that the primary constituencies for libertarianism at any one time would be those individuals and social groups most under attack by the presently existing state and who are consequently most likely to take action against the state, and have the least to lose and the most to gain from the demise of the state. Still wider implications can be drawn from this observation. For instance, a serious anti-state movement will have a natural bias towards the lower socioeconomic orders, given that these bear the brunt of the state's wrath and predations under virtually any kind of political arrangements. Additionally, a serious

---

14   Jerome Tuccille, *It Usually Begins With Ayn Rand,* Twenty-Fifth Anniversary Edition, (Fox and Wilkes, 1997).

libertarian will look very askance at war and military offensiveness given the historic role of this in strengthening and glorifying the state and inflicting still greater oppression, hardship, suffering and death on those already most under the iron heel of the state.

When discussing the relationship between libertarianism and cultural leftism, it is necessary to make an honest attempt to establish a definition of the cultural Left in the first place. Reduced to its lowest common denominator, the cultural Left is a movement that is inclined to favor some demographic groups over others, on the grounds that these groups are somehow more oppressed, victimized or deserving of sympathy than their competitors, along with a wider set of values that tends to favor egalitarianism over elitism, universalism over the particular, internationalism over nationalism, secularism over religion, and cosmopolitanism over traditionalism. Within the context of domestic American or European politics, the cultural Left indicates a bias towards racial and ethnic minorities, feminist women (the position of non-feminist women in the eyes of the Left is more tenuous), homosexuals (and, by extension, bisexuals, transsexuals, and *transgendered* persons), and immigrants (or at least those immigrants originating from the Third World). These are the most obvious examples. Others include atheists, agnostics, *secular humanists,* proponents of religious ecumenicalism, and religious minorities, or at least those with left-wing political views or comprised to a significant degree of persons of non-European ethnicity. Still others are cultural minorities that might be considered *non-traditional,* with a bias towards those like hippies and punk rockers (who generally hold left-wing political views) as opposed to those like bikers and skinheads who are just as likely to identify with the political Right. In a wider socioeconomic sense, there is a cultural bias among leftists towards educated urban professionals over the traditional working class and rural people (particularly white people from these classes), labor unions over business interests, environmentalists over property owners and the *public,* i.e., state sector over the private sector.

The core questions that emerge when examining a potential relationship between libertarianism and the cultural Left are these: How oppressed by the state or by society at large are those demographic groups favored by the Left compared to other groups? How inclined are those groups favored by the Left towards libertarian values? What is the likely standing of groups favored by the Left with regards to the state in the foreseeable future? How valuable are groups favored by the Left likely to be in a future struggle against the state?

On the matter of racism, can it really be said at the present juncture in American history that African-Americans qua African-Americans are oppressed in any special way that is not also experienced by many other groups? Black Americans are only 12.5 percent of the U.S. population, and there is obviously a lengthy history of oppression of blacks by whites in America, yet a black man has been elected President of the United States. The highest ranking diplomat and Cabinet member in the U.S. government under the ostensibly *conservative* Bush administration was a black woman. A black man sits on the U.S. Supreme Court and is in fact the court's most conservative member! Blacks sit in Congress and in state legislatures, hold positions as judges, lawyers, journalists, academics, prominent entertainers and athletes, business executives, police chiefs and many other positions of prominence. Many American cities, where blacks are a numerical majority, have black mayors or black-dominated city governments. American blacks are one half of one percent of the world's population, yet generate ten percent of the world's income. The average standard of living of American blacks is higher than ninety percent of the world's population. If black Americans were an independent nation, they would be the tenth wealthiest nation in the world. [15]

Similar arguments could be made concerning the position of women in American society. [16] The gray area in these matters may be more extensive when it comes to homosexuals, but every American city of any size has a thriving gay subculture and one of the most prominent U.S. Congressmen is an open homosexual, as are many popular celebrities. No doubt some individuals remain who would not give a homosexual a fair shake no matter what, but this is hardly the cultural norm at present and will likely be even less so in the future. [17]

Where is the evidence that anti-racists, feminists, gay liberationists, counterculturalists, multiculturalists, environmentalists or labor unions are generally sympathetic to liberty in any way that distinguishes them from other cultural or demographic groups? Do anti-racists simply argue that the state should remain uninvolved in racial matters and that members of races should be free from

15 Dennis Kimbro, Creating the Millionaire Mind, The Black Collegian. Archived at http://www.black-collegian.com/issues/Gradissue07/millionaire_0607.htm

16 Linda Chavez, Glass Ceiling is a Myth: Reality is Women Make Different Choices, Milwaukee Sentinel, March 25, 1995.

17 Justin Raimondo, Civil Rights for Gays? Free Market, Vol. 14 No. 1, Mises Institute, January 1996.

persecution by the state in ways typified by the Nuremberg laws, South African apartheid and *Jim Crow,* or private racist violence such as that identified with the Ku Klux Klan? This is hardly the case. Anti-racists, almost to a person, are advocates of all sorts of statist intervention into society for the sake of achieving desired levels of racial integration. At a minimum, they tend to insist on statist interference with freedom of association, freedom of contract and private property rights in favor of compulsory integration. They also tend to favor the use of an overarching central government for the purpose of preventing local communities from enacting perceived racist policies, no matter how dubious, marginal, mild or moderate. Indeed, most anti-racist activists favor rather extravagant levels of intervention of many different kinds for the sake of advancing their ideals. It could be argued that *racists* who simply wish to be left alone to practice racial exclusionism within the context of their own separatist enclaves and private associations are (relatively speaking) more libertarian than proponents of extensive interference in local communities and non-state institutions by the central government for the sake of advancing racial liberalism. [18]

What are the libertarian credentials of feminists? To be sure, there are feminists who are also libertarians, such as Wendy McElroy and Sharon Presley in the present day or Voltairine De Cleyre and Emma Goldman from past times, but are such libertarian feminists *normal* among feminists taken as a whole? Frequently, when I have heard feminists speak of *women's issues,* I have inquired as to what exactly *women's issues* are. The first thing that almost always comes up is *abortion rights.* Abortion prohibition may well be as unworkable as alcohol and drug prohibition, but there is no evidence that re-criminalization of abortion is likely occur in the U.S. at any time in the foreseeable future. A referendum for the prohibition of abortion in all but the most exceptional cases recently failed in the highly conservative state of South Dakota. This serves as powerful evidence that the struggle for abortion rights has essentially been won, and that the *pro-choice* cause is not exactly an emergency issue at present. Either way, most pro-choice feminists do not simply advocate that abortion remain decriminalized. They typically advocate direct state funding of abortions, and usually by the central government. Other *women's issues* typically includes such demands as *equal pay for equal work.* Perhaps this is a noble ideal in its own right, but even if one accepts the dubious claim that gender disparity in remuneration rates

---

18   James T. Patterson, Brown v. Board of Education: *A Civil Rights Milestone and Its Troubled Legacy,* (New York: Oxford University Press, 2001).

is derived mostly from a misogynistic conspiracy, it hardly follows that the setting of wages by the state is the appropriate libertarian solution, but it is the frequently proposed feminist solution. Feminists are also frequently found among the ranks of those favoring censorship of sexually explicit literature and the persecution of sex workers or their associates by the state. Laws prohibiting women from voting, engaging in professions or pursuing education were repealed decades ago, and there is no constituency for such legislation today. How then are feminists identifiable enemies of the state in any particular sense? [19]

One might be inclined to think that surely proponents of *gay liberation* must have solid libertarian credentials. Well, not exactly. I recall an angry email I once received from a *gay rights* attorney and law professor associated with the ACLU in response to an article I had written endorsing the presidential candidacy of Ron Paul. What was this fellow's beef with Ron Paul? He was incensed that Ron Paul opposes federal antidiscrimination laws for homosexuals, as if federal antidiscrimination laws were some inalienable natural or constitutional right akin to freedom of speech or freedom of religion. Whenever I have asked *gay rights* activists exactly what *gay rights* would involve, the response usually includes much, much more than the demand that homosexual relationships not be subject to criminalization through so-called *sodomy* laws, or that gay oriented businesses and clubs not be subject to harassment by the police or zoning and liquor licensing boards, or that individual homosexuals should be free from *fag-bashing* violence or less than civil treatment from other individuals, or even for the rights of homosexuals to legally marry (interestingly, the cultural left does not appear to have the same level of zeal for polygamy as same-sex marriage). Instead, at least a substantial portion of the *gay rights* movement advocates further erosions of freedom of association, contract, privacy and private property with antidiscrimination laws, direct subsidies to homosexual organizations, the use of gay marriage laws to require taxpayers to finance state-funded benefits for same-sex couples, granting homosexual pairs equal if not preferential consideration so far as the adoption of children is concerned, criminalizing speech that is critical of homosexuality, the use of tax-funded public schools for the dissemination of pro-gay propaganda under the guise of *sex education* and *teaching tolerance*, enacting *hate crimes* (thought crimes) laws granting homosexuals legal protection above and beyond

---

19   Bob Black, Feminism as Fascism, 1983. Archived at http://www.inspiracy.com/black/abolition/feminism.html

that of ordinary crime victims and many other such privileges. How is this any different from, say, right-wing Christians, organized racists or advocates of *family values* demanding similar favoritism? [20]

How are environmentalists libertarians? There are few political factions around who are quite as state-friendly as these. Of course, there are exceptions such as some *green* decentralists and neo-Luddites. [21] Environmental radicals and other similar factions, such as *animal rights* activists, have at times been the target of state repression, but no more so than pro-life radicals, religious fundamentalist sects or racists. As one who is sympathetic to the ideas of anarcho-syndicalism and a former member of the Industrial Workers of the World (*Wobblies*) it pains me considerably to criticize or attack labor unions, but the issue has to be confronted. Do labor unions in any way take a consistently anti-statist or libertarian line? Or do unions typically prefer privilege for their own members at the expense of other workers? The current support of the auto workers unions for another *bailout* of the automobile industry, whereby unions hope to acquire a share of this particular corporate welfare expenditure, with the costs being shifted onto the wider working classes as a whole, is an excellent case in point. [22]

A similar critique could be made of virtually every other left-wing political interest group. The question also arises of to what degree the Left's coalition of victim groups allied with cultural and intellectual elites and educated professionals is a stable one. For instance, can the modern Left's program of feminism, gay rights, abortion rights and secularism be successfully reconciled with other aspects of the left-wing agenda, such as the importation of ever-increasing numbers of Third World immigrants into Western societies and the granting of disproportionate amounts of political power to indigenous racial minorities, who tend to embrace social conservatism to a greater degree than the white majority? [23] As the constituent groups of the center-left continue to gain political power, it is highly likely that these constituencies will become even less oppositional in nature, more

---

20   Justin Raimondo, Gay Victimology and the Gay Kulturkampf, Anti-State.Com, May 19, 2001. Archived at http://www.anti-state.com/raimondo/raimondo1.html

21   Kirkpatrick Sale, Human Scale, (Perigee, 1982).

22   Elana Schor, Big Three U.S. Car Firms Unlikely to Get Bailout, *The Guardian*, November 17, 2008.

23   Bruce Bawer, Anatomy of Surrender, *City Journal*, Vol. 18 No. 2, Spring 2008.

establishment-friendly and even more statist than they are at present. It is also likely that greater political success will result in a fracturing of the left-wing coalition along ideological, cultural, ethnic, and class lines. Examples might include not only the conflict between white cultural liberals and socially conservative minorities, but also the black bourgeoisie versus the black underclass, black racial nationalists and separatists versus liberal integrationists, affluent professional class women and homosexuals versus the lower socioeconomic orders, the urban liberal-bourgeoisie versus the urban underclass, immigrants versus indigenous racial minorities and many other potential conflicts.

In advancing the struggle against the state, it is strategically advantageous for libertarians to establish what might be called a *hierarchy of priorities*. This means libertarians should single out the most pernicious actions of the state at present as the focus of attack. A rather powerful argument can be made that libertarian energies should be focused on combating military aggression by the present American regime, its ever-expanding domestic police state, and the assortment of economic policies that are collectively having the effect of reducing the economic standing of American working people to eventual Third World levels. This also means developing an understanding of the nature of the particular kind of state libertarians are up against, including such matters as its internal dynamics, demographic relations and ideological superstructure. It would not have done much good for citizens of the Soviet Union or the Eastern European nations in the 1970s to rail against czarism, given that czarism bore no relation to the actually existing state of that particular time period, and that czarism was in fact viewed as an enemy ideology by existing state authorities. Likewise, in politically correct twenty-first century North America it serves no useful purpose to perpetually rail against, for example, *racism, sexism and homophobia* as though we were in Germany circa 1933, Mississippi circa 1957, South Africa circa 1976 or contemporary Saudi Arabia, or to focus our critique of the state on those expressions of the state, such as communism or fascism, whose ideological proponents are on the fringes of American society. Virtually all educated people in the modern world recognize the illegitimacy of traditional forms of totalitarianism, whether from the Left or Right, and of older, more archaic expressions of the state such as aristocracy, theocracy, absolute monarchy or military dictatorship. It is only so-called *democracy* that is considered legitimate and not just any kind of democracy, but centralized mass democracy fused with egalitarian-universalist-multiculturalist ideology, the bureaucratic apparatus of therapeutic-managerialism, and the welfare state.

Therefore, it is *democracy* in this particular form that should be the focus of our ideological assaults. [24]

With this idea in mind, what kind of state will we in the Unites States be facing in the future, and what will be its guiding ideological principles? Historical and demographic patterns indicate that the Republican coalition that emerged triumphant in 1968 and in subsequent decades has just about run out of steam. It is likely that the Democrats and, by extension, the center-left will emerge as the dominant national party in the years ahead with the support base of the Democrats rooted in expanding racial minority and immigrant populations, the soon-to-be elderly 1960s generation, the increasingly powerful feminist and gay movements, an expanded class of educated urban professionals, environmentalists, urban blue-collar Catholics and *white ethnics,* and enough WASPish middle class centrists and liberals to maintain an electoral majority.[25] At the same time, the American political and economic system has become increasingly militarist, imperialist, corporatist and police statist in recent decades and there is no sign this will discontinue under Democratic rule. There was certainly no discontinuation of these trends under the reign of Bill Clinton and there is no evidence that a ruling party composed of the likes of Charles Schumer, Hillary Clinton, Joe Biden and Dianne Feinstein will be any more benevolent, competent, restrained or fair-minded that the Bush Republicans have been. In other words, what we will soon have in the United States is a multiethnic, multicultural, secular, feminized and gayized political class presiding over a crumbling imperialist empire and decaying corporatist economy. This ruling class will have at its disposal a massive police state apparatus that has been built up in recent decades under the guise of the wars on drugs, crime and terrorism.

Further social and economic deterioration will likely generate increased social unrest, and the ruling class will respond by attempting to tighten the grip. We can expect that the state will continue to become increasingly pernicious, and justify its actions in the name of supposed liberal ideals, given center-left ideological dominance. Remember how Janet Reno justified the massacre at Waco in the name of combating child abuse and right-wing, religious fundamentalist,

---

24   Hans Hermann Hoppe, *Democracy: The God That Failed,* (Transaction Publishers, 2001)

25   John B. Judis and Ruy Teixeira, *The Emerging Democratic Majority,* (Scribner, 2004).

gun nuts? This synthesis of liberal ideology and fascist methodology might be properly described as *totalitarian humanism*.[26]

So the most relevant future political question for libertarians will be, *How do we go about combating the totalitarian humanist state?* If the center-left is likely to be politically dominant in the future, it naturally follows that a viable anti-state resistance would have a certain *conservative* dimension to it. Yet this *conservative* aspect would function only as a component part of a wider strategy that is simultaneously libertarian, populist, pluralist and class-based. Such a movement would be libertarian, in the sense of defending all groups who come under attack by the state, irrespective of their particular beliefs or cultural background. These could sometimes include groups favored by the Left to be sure, such as transvestites subject to police harassment or urban racial minorities imprisoned en masse under the guise of the *war on drugs* and the related prison-industrial complex. Yet it might also include groups despised by the Left, including social conservatives, religious fundamentalists, ethnic preservationists, cultural traditionalists, tax resisters, *racists*, odd religious sects or cults, firearms enthusiasts, motorcycle clubs, Holocaust *revisionists* and other *politically incorrect* persons who fall prey to the repressive apparatus of the state. It would no doubt include still other groups ignored or despised by both Left and Right, including drug users, prisoners, prostitutes and other sex workers, truants (*school resisters*), psychiatric inmates, indigenous people, the homeless, the physically disabled, the mentally ill, gang members or racial nationalists among the minority groups. It would be populist in the sense of positioning itself as a movement of the people against the elites. It would be pluralist, in the sense of recognition and inclusion of a diversity of cultural identities out of political necessity and out of recognition of the legitimacy of Otherness. It would be class-based in the sense of having a primary economic orientation towards the lumpenproletariat (the urban underclass), the petite bourgeoisie (small businessmen and the self-employed), the neo-peasantry (small farmers and rural agricultural workers), the *déclassé* elements (persons from the middle to upper classes who reject their class values of their class of origin), and the dispossessed middle class that is rapidly sinking into the ranks of the underclass.

It is clear enough that those who are most under attack by the state and those from the socioeconomic groups that might be said to

---

26   Keith Preston, The New Totalitarianism, LewRockwell.Com, January 22, 2007. Archived at http://www.lewrockwell.com/orig8/preston1.html

be the *vanguard classes* of the struggle against state-capitalism display many considerable cultural, religious, racial, ethnic and regional differences among themselves. The implication of this for the relationship of libertarianism to cultural matters is that serious libertarian opponents of the state and its institutional tentacles would necessarily be advocates of neither *cultural conservatism* nor *cultural leftism,* but would instead display a bias towards an authentic cultural pluralism, primarily by recognizing the right to sovereignty and self-determination of a variety of cultural groups, many of whom may be in conflict with regards to core cultural values. It is crucial that a distinction be made between meta-political structures, which may contain within themselves a myriad of cultural forms, and the specific cultural orientations of individuals and particular groups. A libertarianism that positioned itself as a genuine *third way* in opposition to both the totalitarian humanist Left and the plutocratic-corporatist Right and appealed to all those under attack by the state across the cultural spectrum would likely attract at least some level of sympathy from an unusual assortment of demographic groups. These might include elements of the populist *far right,* including persons with quite conservative value systems, refugees from *middle America* who are culturally mainstream but have been politically and economically radicalized due to their deteriorating situation, socially conservative but politically radical racial minorities, the sectors of the *far left* and the counterculture that exist outside of the totalitarian humanist paradigm, the lower socioeconomic sectors of the center-left constituent groups who will likely splinter from the bourgeoisie elite within their own demographic milieu at some point in the future, rebellious youth inclined towards political radicalism, or the urban lumpenproletarian class of ordinary street criminals.[27]

While thick libertarianism is correct in many of its core insights, such as the view that libertarianism requires a wider cultural foundation or should be connected to values beyond simple anti-statism itself, thick libertarianism also fails on certain levels to adopt the values and priorities necessary for a successful effort at combating the state in a modern liberal-democratic / state-capitalist / totalitarian humanist society. Rather, thick libertarianism in its present form would likely suffer the same fate as the New Left of the 1960s, eventually becoming incorporated into the wider framework of state-capitalism and

---

27   Keith Preston, Liberty and Populism: Building An Effective Resistance Movement for North America, (American Revolutionary Vanguard, 2006). Archived at http://attackthesystem.com/liberty-and-populism-building-an-effective-resistance-movement-for-north-america/

American imperialism in exchange for ruling class recognition of its social and cultural agenda (which at present differs very little from American and other Western cultural and intellectual elites). The causes of anti-racism, feminism, gay liberation, counterculturalism, multiculturalism and environmentalism have advanced considerably over the past four decades. Yet the state has grown ever more expansive, expensive, intrusive and totalitarian. The police state in particular has experienced an explosive growth rate. The corporatist economy has tightened its grip considerably and the position of the poor and working class is on a downward spiral. Under the doctrines of global hegemony, preventative war, the *war on terrorism,* the *global democratic revolution* and military humanism, the state currently displays a more brazen commitment to militarism and aggressive warfare than ever before. Clearly, an ascendant cultural leftism has been powerless to prevent such occurrences. Members of demographic groups favored by the Left have proven to be just as corrupt, tyrannical, venal or incompetent once given political power as any of their *straight white male* predecessors.

What might be some *thick* values, while irrelevant to the coercive authority of the state per se, that might be helpful as part of a broader foundation for combating actually existing states of the kind found in the contemporary First World?

A defense of the sovereignty of particular nations against imperialism, multi-national nation-states, and international quasi-governmental bodies.

A defense of the sovereignty of local communities and regional cultures against the power of overarching central governments.

Ethno-pluralism or the view that each unique ethnic group should have a territory where it is a demographic majority and with a political system representative of its cultural foundations. The Swiss canton system may well be the most advanced model of this type of any system currently in practice.

The view that cultural differences are best dealt with according to the principles of individual liberty, voluntary association, pluralism and peaceful co-existence where possible, yet where this is not possible localism, decentralism, secessionism, separatism and mutual self-segregation are likely the most preferable alternatives.

A distinction between natural or voluntary hierarchies and authorities, and coercive or artificial ones.

Recognition of the iron law of oligarchy, or the view that elites are inevitable, and an emphasis on meritocracy, as opposed to simply tearing down all authorities, institutions, and organizations, thereby creating a power vacuum that allows the worst to get to the top.

Recognition of the legitimacy of Otherness, and an understanding that true *tolerance* is not simply tolerating people one likes, but tolerating those whom one finds personally repulsive. Just as toleration of the Other is not synonymous with approval or agreement, so does tolerance of one's self by the Other not grant the right to demand approval.

Recognition of the inherent inequality of persons, groups, cultures, nations, etc. and that effort to impose artificial or unnatural equality can only result in tyranny, chaos or stagnation.

Adherence to what traditionalist Catholics call the *subsidiarity principle*, meaning that problems are best dealt with on a decentralized basis by those closest to them, rather than on the basis of abstract solutions imposed from above.

Application of the insights of modern social psychology, which indicates that most people are herd creatures, and inevitably get their sense of *right and wrong* not from any innate sense of conscience or a rational evaluation of available facts, but according to cues taken from leaders, peers and perceived sources of cultural authority.

Recognition of the value of intermediary institutions, such as families, communities, voluntary associations, independent business and labor organizations, charities, philanthropies, private schools and universities, cultural organizations, and even private citizens' militias as a bulwark against the all-encompassing authoritarian presence of the state, and the need to defend the sovereignty and legitimacy of such institutions.

Recognition of Acton's dictum that *power corrupts and absolute power corrupts absolutely.*

What I have outlined here is certainly not *conservatism*, at least not as understood in conventional American political terminology. Such an outlook would have no interest in maintaining the American empire and would regard right-wing jingoists of the kind common to afternoon talk-radio with contempt. It would give no support to upholding the interests of the state-capitalist *big business* elites and would dismiss the *religious right* as know-nothing ignoramuses operating as stooges for the right-wing of big capital and the Israel Lobby. Nor would it have the *cops walk on water* mentality common to *law and order* conservatives or the hysterical Puritanism concerning issues like sex and drugs common to some social conservatives. This movement would share conventional conservatism's interest in reducing government taxing and spending, but in a radically different way from that championed by the mainstream Republican Party-oriented Right. Instead, a comprehensive libertarianism of the kind being suggested would pursue the goal of reducing or eliminating government intervention into the economy in a way that is compatible with the interests of those classes previously identified as the vanguard of the struggle.

Nor would this movement constitute *leftism* as conventionally understood. Instead, this new radicalism would regard government taxation, regulation and redistribution with suspicion, and apply the insights of such thinkers as Gabriel Kolko that the regulatory welfare state is a means of eliminating smaller competitors to big capital, co-opting labor and pacifying the poor. It would not share the Cultural Marxism of the Left, which regards virtually the whole history of Western civilization as one big racist, sexist, homophobic, xenophobic, anti-Semitic, ethnocentric, colonialist conspiracy, but would instead recognize that it is indeed the heritage of liberal Western civilization, rooted in the intellectual culture of the classical Greco-Roman civilization of antiquity that found its renewal in the Renaissance and the Enlightenment, and its political expression in English liberalism and the American Revolution, that provides us with the very cultural foundation necessary to make libertarianism possible.[28] Nor would it champion liberal or Marxist universalism, instead recognizing that libertarianism and its wider civilization foundations are uniquely Western in origin, and while other cultures and civilizations may have overlapping traditions of their own, there is no need for us to export our ways into their societies, nor theirs into ours. Consequently, the

---

28   William S. Lind, The Origins of Political Correctness, Accuracy in Academia. Archived at http://www.academia.org/lectures/lind1.html

45

foreign policy outlook of this kind of libertarian movement would seek to neither maintain foreign nations as client states nor impose Western standards of *democracy* or *human rights* on other cultures. Let the residents of Asia, Africa and Latin America do as they wish so long as they don't bother us (and, in return, we won't bother them).[29]

No discussion of libertarian politics can be complete without some mention of practical strategic considerations as well as abstract, theoretical ones. If it is the state and its emanations that are to be attacked, and if it is the center-left and the corresponding system of totalitarian humanism that forms the ideological superstructure of the actually existing state, then it follows that the foundation of a viable anti-state movement in the future will be rooted in the populist right, radical middle, extreme left, and the lumpenproletariat as all of these are outside the totalitarian humanist paradigm and under attack in one way or another by the state. The next step will be to splinter and neutralize the center-left by splitting its constituent groups along cultural, economic, class and ideological lines of the kind previously mentioned. Beyond that, there is the need for a healthy balance between populism and elitism. Until recently, the mainstream Right managed to advance itself politically with appeals to nationalism, economic conservatism and cultural populism.[30] If this is no longer viable, and it appears that it may not be, then the logical alternative would be economic populism (*the people* verses *big government* and *big business*), cultural libertarianism (a *leave me alone* coalition) and a Jeffersonian version of decentralist patriotism with emphasis on local and regional sovereignty and identities within the context of the American revolutionary tradition.

Libertarians should aspire to be the elite leadership corps of a larger, broad-based populist movement that encourages the development of local sovereignty and secession movements in opposition to the central government and the empire. Given that the majority of the U.S. population lives in approximately one hundred large metropolitan areas, a class-based radicalism would essentially pit the urban poor and working classes and their natural allies (the so-called *red state rubes*, the lower to lower middle classes from the rural areas and smaller towns) against the urban liberal-bourgeoisie elite who staff and maintain the managerial bureaucracy on behalf of

---

29 Noam Chomsky, *The New Military Humanism*, (Common Courage Press, 2002).

30 Donald T. Critchlow, *The Conservative Ascendency: How the GOP Right Made Political History*, (Harvard University Press, 2007).

the plutocracy. The political arrangements likely to emerge from the victory of such a radical movement would involve a kind of cultural separatism. Culturally conservative rural communities, small towns, *red states* and elsewhere would be free to separate themselves from the perceived ills of *liberal* society as would socially conservative urban racial minorities, Muslims and others who might also have their own separatist enclaves. Yet independent metropolitan city-states would likely remain as cosmopolitan in nature as they are now, perhaps more so, as the expulsion of the state and the overthrow of the plutocracy should bring with it greatly expanded economic opportunities with urban areas becoming even greater centers of trade and cultural exchange than they are now. Minus the overarching authority of the federal government or the influence of socially conservative or religiously fundamentalist rural counties and small towns, urban centers could begin to experiment with many of the radically anti-authoritarian ideas favored by libertarians and decentralists, such as drug decriminalization, citizen militias, common law courts, restitution-based penal systems, the abolition of compulsory education, a free-market in health care (including alternative health care and prescription medicines), expanded rights of self-defense, non-state social services, alternative media, the elimination of zoning ordinances, the repeal of the drinking age and other *victimless crime* laws, urban farming and so on.

From where have the greatest acts of resistance to the state emerged in the last twenty years? One of these was certainly the so-called *L.A. riots* of 1992, a massive rebellion that was misguided in many ways, but rooted in resistance to police brutality.[31] Another was the militia movement of the 1990s, which emerged in response to the federal massacres at Waco and Ruby Ridge. Still another was the *Battle of Seattle* of 1999 pitting a wide assortment of lumpen elements against the police in protest against the plutocracy. More recently, there was the Ron Paul campaign with its libertarian, populist and antiwar themes. It is efforts such as these that provide the models and foundations for a revolutionary anti-state movement on which libertarians should build.

---

31 Anonymous, The Rebellion in Los Angeles: The Context of a Proletarian Uprising, 1992. Archived at http://attackthesystem.com/the-rebellion-in-los-angeles-the-context-of-a-proletarian-uprising/

5

The Myth of the Rule of Law and the Future of Repression

Richard Spencer's article, "Obama's Enabling Act." raises some interesting questions regarding the significance of the recently passed National Defense Authorization Act, and its probable impact, that I believe merit further discussion. The editorial issued on December 17 by the editors of *Taki's Magazine*, "The Government v. Everyone," represents fairly well the shared consensus of critics of the NDAA whose ranks include conservative constitutionalists and left-wing civil libertarians alike. While I share the opposition to the Act voiced by these critics, I also believe that Richard is correct to point out the questionable presumptions regarding legal and constitutional theory and alarmist rhetoric that have dominated the critics' arguments.

Wholesale abrogation of core provisions of the U.S. Constitution is hardly rare in American history. The literature of leftist or libertarian historians of American politics is filled with references to the Alien and Sedition Act, Lincoln's assumption of dictatorial powers during the Civil War, the repression of the labor movement during WWI, the internment of the Japanese during WW2 and so forth. Mainstream liberal critics of these aspects of American history will lament the manner by which America supposedly strays so frequently from her high-minded ideals, whereas more radical leftist critics will insist such episodes illustrate what a rotten society America always was right from the beginning.

Meanwhile, conservatives will lament how the noble, almost god-like efforts of the revered "Founding Fathers" have been perverted and destroyed by subsequent generations of evil or misguided liberals, socialists, atheists, or whomever, thereby plunging the nation into the present dark era of big government and moral decadence. These systems of political mythology notwithstanding, a more realist-driven analysis of the history of the actual practice of American statecraft might conclude that such instances of the state stepping outside of its own proclaimed ideals or breaking its own rules transpire because, well, that's what states do.

The Myth of the Rule of Law and the Future of Repression

Carl Schmitt considered the essence of politics to be the existence of organized collectives with the potential to engage in lethal conflict with one another. Max Weber defined the state as an entity claiming a monopoly on the legitimate use of violence. Schmitt's dictum, *"Sovereign is he who decides on the state of exception,"* indicates there must be some ultimate rule-making authority that decides what constitutes "legitimacy" and what does not, and that this sovereign entity is consequently not bound by its own rules. This principle is descriptive rather than prescriptive or normative in nature. Schmitt's conception of the political is simply an analysis of "how things work" as opposed to "what ought to be."

Like all other political collectives, the United States possesses a body of political mythology whose function is to convey legitimacy upon its own state. For Americans, this mythology takes on the form of what Robert Bellah identified as the "civil religion." The tenets of this civil religion grant Americans a unique and exceptional place in history as the Promethean purveyors of "freedom," "democracy," "equality," "opportunity," or some other supposedly noble ideal. According to this mythology, America takes on the role of a providential nation that is in some way particularly favored by either a vague, deist-like divine force (Jefferson's "nature's god") in the mainstream politico-religious culture, or the biblical god in the case of the evangelicals, or the progressive forces of history for left-wing secularists. The Declaration of Independence and the Constitution are the sacred writings of the American civil religion. It is no coincidence that constitutional fundamentalists and religious fundamentalists are often the same people. Prominent "founding fathers" such as Washington or Madison assume the role of prophets or patriarchs akin to Moses and Abraham.

In American political and legal culture, this civil religion and body of political mythology becomes intertwined with the liberal myth of the "rule of law." According to this conception, "law" takes on an almost mystical quality and the Constitution becomes a kind of magical artifact (like the genie's lantern) whose invocation will ostensibly ward off tyrants. This legal mythology is often expressed through slogans such as *"We should be a nation of laws and not men"* (as though laws are somehow codified by forces or entities other than mere mortal humans) and public officials caught acting outside strict adherence to legal boundaries are sometimes vilified for violation of "the rule of law." (I recall comical pieties of this type being expressed during the Iran-Contra scandal of the late 1980s.) Ultimately, of course, there is no such thing as "the rule of law." There is only the rule of the "sovereign." The law is always subordinate to the sovereign rather than vice versa. Schmitt's conception of the political indicates that the world is comprised first and foremost of brawling collectives struggling on behalf of each of their existential prerogatives. The practice of politics amounts to street-gang warfare *writ large* where the overriding principle becomes "protect one's turf!" rather than "rule of law".

As an aside, I am sometimes asked how my general adherence to Schmittian political theory can be reconciled with my anarchist beliefs. However, it was my own anarchism that initially attracted me to the thought of Schmitt. His recognition of the essence of the political as organized collectives with the potential to engage in lethal conflict and his understanding of sovereignty as exemption from the rule-making authority of the state have the ironic effect of stripping away and destroying the systems of mythology on which states are built. Schmitt's analysis of the nature of the state is so penetrating that it gives the game away. Politics is simply about maintaining power. Period.

Another irony is that Schmitt helped to clarify my anarchist beliefs considerably. I adhere to the dictionary definition of anarchism as the goal of replacing the state with a confederation or agglomeration of voluntary communities (while recognizing a certain degree of subjectivity to the question of what is "voluntary" and what is not). Theoretically, anarchist communities could certainly reflect the values of ideological anarchists like Kropotkin, Rothbard, or Dorothy Day. But such communities could also be organized on the model of South Africa's Orania, or traditionalist communities like the Hasidim or Amish, or fringe cultural elements like UFO true-believers. Paradoxically, such communities could otherwise reflect the "normal" values of Middle America (minus the state).

The concept of fourth generation warfare provides a key insight as to how political anarchism can be reconciled with the political theory of Carl Schmitt. According to fourth generation theory as it has been outlined by Martin Van Creveld and William S. Lind, the state is in the process of receding as the loyalties of populations are being transferred to other entities such as religions, tribes, ideological movements, gangs, cults, paramilitaries, or whatever. Scenarios are emerging with increasing frequency where such non-state actors engage in warfare with states or in the place of states. Lebanon's Hezbollah, which has essentially replaced the Lebanese state as both the defender of the nation and as the provider of necessary services on which the broader population depends, is a standard model of a fourth generation entity.

In other words, Hezbollah has *replaced the state as the sovereign entity in Lebanese society.*

Another example is Columbia's FARC, which has likewise dislodged the Colombian state as the sovereign in FARC-controlled territorial regions. The implication of this for political anarchism is that for the anarchist goal of autonomous, voluntary communities to succeed, a non-state entity (or collection of entities) must emerge that is capable of protecting the communities from conquest or subversion and possesses the will to do so. In other words, for anarchism to work there must be in place the equivalent of an anarchist version of Hezbollah that replaces the state as the sovereign in the wider society, probably in the form of a decentralized militia confederation similar to that organized by the Anarchists of Catalonia during the Spanish Civil War...in case anyone was wondering.

The Future of Repression

Dealing with more immediate questions, the passage of the National Defense Authorization Act raises the issue of to what level repression carried out by the American state in the future will be taken, and of what particular form this repression will assume. I agree with Richard that it is improbable that NDAA represents any significant change of direction or dramatic acceleration in these areas. Therefore, it is highly unlikely that American political dissidents (the readers of AlternativeRight.Com, for instance) will be subject to mass arrests and indefinite detention without trial. Such tactics are likely to be reserved for individuals, primarily foreigners, genuinely involved or believed to be involved in the planning of acts of actual terrorism against American targets. There is at present very little of that within the context of domestic American society.

However, the unwarranted nature of Alex Jones-style alarmism does not mean there is no danger on the horizon. What is needed is a healthy medium between panic and complacency. Richard has argued that our present systems of soft totalitarianism that we find in the contemporary Western world may well give way to hard totalitarianism as Cultural Marxism/Totalitarian Humanism continues to tighten its grip. While this is a concern that I share and a prophecy that I regrettably think has a considerable chance of fulfillment, the question arises of what form "hard" totalitarianism might take in the future of the West.

The Tyranny of the Politically Correct

It is unlikely we will ever develop states in the West that are organized on the classical totalitarian model complete with over the top pageantry and heads of states with strange uniforms and facial hair, given the way in which these are inimical to the universalist ideology, globalist ambitions, commercial interests, and aesthetic values of Western elites. Rather, I suspect the future of Western repression will take on either one of two forms (or perhaps a combination of both).

One of these is a model where repression rarely involves long term imprisonment or state-sponsored lethal action against dissidents. Instead, such repression might take on the form of persistent and arbitrary harassment, or the ongoing escalation of the use of professional and economic sanctions, targeting the families and associates of dissidents, or the petty criminalization of those who speak or act in defiance of establishment ideology. Richard has discussed the recent events involving Emma West and David Duke, as well as his own treatment at the hands of the Canadian authorities, and I suspect it is state action of this type that will largely define Western repression in the foreseeable future.

The state may not murder you or put you in prison for decades without trial, but you may lose your job, have your professional licenses revoked or the social service authorities threaten to remove your children from your home, or be subject to significant but brief harassment by legal authorities. You may find yourself brought up on minor criminal charges (akin to those that might be levied against a shoplifter or a pot smoker) if you utter the wrong words. Likewise, the state will increasingly look the other way as the use of extra-legal violence by leftist and other pro-system thugs is employed against dissenters. Indeed, much of what I have outlined here is already taking place and it can be expected that such incidents will become much more frequent and severe in the years and decades ahead. What I have outlined in this paragraph largely defines the practice of political repression as it currently exists in the West, particularly outside the United States, where traditions upholding free speech do not run quite as deeply.

However, this by no means indicates that Americans are off the hook. An even greater issue of concern, particularly for the United States, involves the convergence of four factors within contemporary American society and statecraft. These are the decline of the American empire in spite of the continuation of America's massive military-industrial complex, mass immigration and radical demographic transformation, rapid economic deterioration and the disappearance of the conventional American middle class, and the growth of the general apparatus of state repression over the last four decades (the prison-industrial complex frequently criticized by the Left, for instance).

The combination of mass Third World immigration and ongoing economic decline, if continued uninterrupted, will have the effect of replicating the traditional Third World model class system in the U.S. (and perhaps much of the West over time). A class system organized on the basis of an opulent few at the top and impoverished many among the masses (the Brazilian model, for instance) will likely be accompanied by escalating social unrest and political instability. Such trends will be ever more greatly exacerbated by growing social, cultural, and ethnic conflict brought about by demographic change.

The American state has at its disposal an enormous military industrial complex that, frankly, wants to remain in business even as foreign military adventures continue to become less politically and economically viable. Likewise, the ongoing domestic wars waged by the American state against drugs, crime, gangs, guns, et. al. have generated a rather large "police industrial complex" with American borders. Libertarian writers such as William Norman Grigg have diligently documented the ongoing process of the militarization of American law enforcement and the continued blurring of distinctions between the rules of engagement involving soldiers on the battlefield on one hand and policemen dealing with civilians on the other. The literature of libertarian critics is filled with horror stories of, for instance, small town mayors having their household pets blown away by SWAT team members during the course of bungled drug raids.

The point is that as economic and social unrest, along with increasingly intense demographic conflict, continues to arise as it likely will in the foreseeable American future, the state will have at its disposal a significant apparatus for the carrying out of genuinely brutal repression of the kind normally associated with Latin American or Middle Eastern countries. Recall, for example, the "disappeared" of Latin America during the 1970s and 1980s. It is not improbable that we dissidents in the totalitarian humanist states of the postmodern West will face a dangerous brush with such circumstances at some point in the future.

6

The Roots of Political Correctness

It is indeed problematic to identify Marxism as a theory that is not rooted in economic determinism and the view of class conflict as the defining element of capitalist society. Marx and Engels themselves had many ideas that would be considered "far right" today, particularly their views on racism and imperialism. Leftist anti-racism really doesn't take off until the post-WW2 era (mostly as a backlash against Nazism, in my view).

Marx and Engels were essentially Germanic or at least Nordic supremacists, who viewed indigenous peoples as non-historical, and regarded Western imperialism as a historically progressive force (they had the same view of capitalism). The early anarchists took an anti-imperialist position but Marxist anti-imperialism really begins with Lenin. At best, the Frankfurt School's "cultural Marxism" is a revision of orthodox Marxism...at the very best. These are among the reasons I prefer the term totalitarian humanism for PC rather than cultural Marxism.

Aspects of political correctness seem to have been imported from Maoist China during the Cultural Revolution era rather than through the Frankfurt School. Remember the reverence that hard core New Left radicals often had for Mao in the late 60s and early 70s. Notice the similarities between a Maoist self-criticism session and the self-flagellation common among adherents of PC.

I don't think the Marxist influenced hard left alone is responsible for the growth of PC. There's also progressive Christianity, and progressivism in general, which has much different roots than Marxism.

This quote:

> *"If humanities faculties are really geared to brainwashing students into accepting the postulates of far-left ideology, the composition of western parliaments and presidencies and the roaring success of corporate capitalism suggests they're doing an astoundingly bad job.*

The Roots of Political Correctness

Anyone who takes a cool look at the last three decades of politics will think it bizarre that anyone could interpret what's happened as the triumph of an all-powerful left."

I would agree that while the totalitarian humanists often have their roots in anti-capitalism, it is certainly true that they have since made their accommodations to capitalism and are now trying to use capitalism to their own ends. See Tomislav Sunic's article "The '68ers" on this. This is not particularly surprising. Totalitarian movements often start out as anti-capitalist but use capitalism as a tool once they obtain power (see Mussolini's fascism, Hitler's NSDAP, and even Lenin's "New Economic Policy.") For that matter, see present day China.

Lastly, PC and capitalism are not necessarily in conflict. Capitalism wants workers, consumers, investors, and new markets. This means operating among an ever greater number of demographics. It is therefore perfectly logical that capitalism would embrace anti-racism, feminism, gay rights, etc. They want to sell products to minorities, women, and gays, and hire them as workers and managers, not discriminate against them. (See Noam Chomsky's comments on how big business supports anti-racism). I suspect the serious thinkers among the cultural Left realize this, which is part of the reason why they have softened their anti-capitalism in their old age. This also explains why the corporate class has mostly rolled over in the face of PC. Remember that Singapore (which the Left considers to be fascist, and which free market conservatives often hold up as a model) also has strict "hate speech" laws.

I think we can interpret this stuff with either a grand narrative or a focused narrative, depending on what direction we want to go.

I would agree that the fanatical political correctness we see coming from the cultural Left today is traceable to Puritanism, but only in the sense that Puritanism emerges due to certain strands in the human personality or human psychology. There's been a great deal of discussion of to what degree modern totalitarianism is an outgrowth of puritan forms of Christianity. Some people have argued that the lineage of PC can be traced directly to old fashioned Calvinist Puritanism, and it's possible to outline a historical trajectory of that kind with a broad brush.

The way it seems to have happened is that Puritanism emerged in the UK and then migrated to North America where it became the basis of the founding New England settlements. Over time, the Enlightenment overruns orthodox Calvinism but the puritan spirit remains and finds its way into neo-Protestant movements like Unitarianism and Progressive Christianity. (If one wants to know what this spirit is like, read the lyrics to the "Battle Hymn of the Republic," the anthem of the Yankees during the American Civil War).

This kind of Progressive Christian neo-Puritanism finds its way into secular progressivism in the 20th century (with movements like Prohibition to use one of many examples), and creates the cultural and intellectual atmosphere for "cultural Marxism" to take root (the latter having been imported from Europe).

Some theorists of the European New Right like Alain de Benoist and Tomislav Sunic have argued that Marxism is a kind of secularization of Christian ideas like original sin (which becomes "alienation" in the Marxist outlook via Jean Jacques Rousseau), dualism, eschatology, egalitarianism, etc. Rothbard made a similar but narrower version of this argument regarding Protestantism as he tended to admire the Catholic emphasis on natural law. Catholic traditionalists like Erik von Kuehnelt Leddihn have actually argued that German Protestantism in the Lutheran tradition was a forerunner to Nazism. I have also seen some Objectivist-influenced philosophers making arguments of this kind. And, of course, there's the Nietzschean critique of slave morality that Nietzsche saw as having Christian roots.

But whatever the validity of these grand narratives, it seems to me we can also develop a more focused narrative. For example, the "privilege theory" that present day leftists (and, rather embarrassingly, left-libertarians) are obsessed with has its roots in American Marxist-Leninist theoreticians who developed the doctrine of "white skin privilege" in the 1960s, which then found its way into the New Left via Maoist groups like the Weather Underground. This privilege theory converged with Marcuse's view that the working class had been bought off by consumer culture and integrated into capitalism. The extreme wing of the New Left adopted the view that the white working class in America had become collaborators with white skin privilege and that the black proletariat was the real revolutionary class. And then other groups like feminists, homosexuals, etc started getting added to this.

Paul Gottfried argues that this stuff took root in the American universities and among the American cultural elite first because the pre-existing cultural atmosphere of neo-Protestant Puritanism had created an intellectual and cultural environment that was susceptible to it. Then the Europeans picked it up and ran with it.

For instance, I've heard it argued that PC takes on a different form in the historically Protestant European countries (i.e. the smug, smarmy moral Puritanism of the progressives) than it does in the historically Catholic countries (where it more closely resembles the anti-fascism of the Old Left, for example, some of the first laws criminalizing Holocaust denial were introduced by the Communist deputies in the French Parliament, and the French CP was the last to de-Stalinize in Western Europe). Of course, Germany is a special case given their history.

As for the Jewish role in all this, it is certainly true that historically speaking a lot of Jewish intellectuals and politicians have been leftists, but so have an awful lot of Anglo-Saxons, Americans, and continental Europeans. I think modern Jewish intellectuals tend to be liberals and leftists because modern intellectuals generally tend to be liberals and leftists. It's true that some Jews have embraced multiculturalism out of the belief that Jews are ostensibly safer in a multi-ethnic society without a dominant ethnic majority. It is also true that Jews were disproportionately represented within the Communist movement, but much of this was more of repudiation than an embrace of Jewish identity. Its seems to me that, at best, liberal, socialist, or multicultural trends among Jews simply converged or ran parallel with trends of this type found among Gentile neo-Protestants or European intellectuals generally.

I would not deny the role of many individual Jews or Jewish organizations in the fostering of political correctness and its predecessors. But I think the question is one of which is the dog and which is the tail? The first problem I have with the "Jew-centric" interpretation of the origins of PC is that it seems that at the very least if "the Jews" are responsible for fostering these kinds of things, they have had a great deal of assistance from the Gentiles along the way. I agree that Jews tend to be overrepresented among both intellectual and socioeconomic elites given their rather small demographic size, but it still seems to me that the currents within Jewish intellectual culture that have contributed to the development of PC have merely been a subset of wider cultural, intellectual, and political currents whose principal figures and movers have been Gentiles. For example, in the US today, WASPish liberal Episcopalians, progressive Lutherans, liberal Catholics, and Reform Jews all have virtually identical views on social and cultural issues. One group is as politically correct as the other. From what I have seen, it is the same way in Europe.

Jewish thinkers were generally sympathetic to the Enlightenment-inspired revolutions of the eighteenth century, but no more so than plenty of left-wing Christians of the era and the liberal European bourgeoisie. There were certainly plenty of Jews in the international Communist movement, and disproportionately so, but I disagree that Communism can be characterized as a Jewish movement per se. Particularly when one considers the actual Nordicism of Marx and Engels, and the fact that Communism traveled so well in cultures where Jews were not particularly present or prominent (e.g. Northern and Eastern Asia). Jews were also prominent in the New Left, and disproportionately so, but a bigger question is why did the New Left happen when it did and in the places that it did? It seems that there was a pre-existing cultural and intellectual environment in which "cultural Marxism" was able to develop via the influence of currents like the Frankfurt School and what might be called "Western Maoism." It seems that Progressive Christianity, rooted in puritanism, and its secular Progressive offspring created this cultural and intellectual environment in American northeastern universities (with this subsequently spreading to the West Coast). And again, there was at the very least plenty of Gentile abetting of the "Jewish influence." For instance, of the two founders of "white skin privilege theory" I mentioned, Noel Ignatiev is/was Jewish. But Ted Allen was a Gentile from the American Midwest. This illustration represents a kind of microcosm of the Jewish and Gentile relationships in most leftist movements.

It has also been argued that "Political Correctness" was first used by the orthodox Marxists, people who followed the Moscow line.

Yes, and it was also found among the more extreme tendencies on the New Left as well, i.e. the Western Maoist groups like the Weather Underground and the Black Liberation Army.

I agree with much of what Paul says here about the influence of the Frankfurt School, and I've written about that myself, as well as promoted William S. Lind's analysis of the Frankfurt School question. But it's interesting that the Frankfurt School ideas first took root in American universities with a lengthy history and legacy of neo-puritan Progressive Christian influence. It seems that the latter paved the way for the former.

Horowitz's claim would make sense, because in my efforts to track the roots of the term, it seems to start appearing in the rhetoric of the Maoist-influenced groups of the New Left. Plus, I've always thought that the Maoist concept of self-criticism was an important influence on the development of political correctness in the West, e.g. white guilt, the idea that no effort to combat "oppression" is ever good enough, neutrality is collaboration, etc. Among leftists today, one will literally observe them holding workshops with titles like "Overcoming White Supremacy in the Anti-Racist Movement" or "Sexism in the LGBTQ Community," and they take all of this very seriously.

7

The Oppression of "Human Rights"

"Whoever invokes humanity wants to cheat."– Pierre Joseph Proudhon

In his important work *Beyond Human Rights: Defending Freedoms* (Arktos, 2011), Alain De Benoist aptly summarizes the first article of faith of the present day secular theocracy which reigns in the Western world:

> One proof of this is its dogmatic character; it cannot be debated. That is why it seems today as unsuitable, as blasphemous, as scandalous to criticize the ideology of human rights as it was earlier to doubt the existence of God. Like every religion, the discussion of human rights seeks to pass off its dogmas as so absolute that one could not discuss them without being extremely, stupid, dishonest, or wicked...(O)ne implicitly places their opponents beyond the pale of humanity, since one cannot fight someone who speaks in the name of humanity while remaining human oneself.

While reading the above passage, I was instantly reminded of a particularly venal leftist critic who once amusingly described me as "flunking out of the human race" for, among other things, promoting the work of Benoist. The zealous religiosity which the apostles of human rights attach to their cause is particularly ironic given the nebulous and imprecise nature of their cherished dogma. As Thomas Szasz has observed:

> Never before in our history have political and popular discourse been so full of rights-talk, as they are today. People appeal to disability rights, civil rights, gay rights, reproduction rights (abortion), the right to choose (also abortion), the right to health care, the right to reject treatment...and so forth, each a rhetorical device to justify one or another social policy and its enforcement by means of the coercive apparatus of the state.

Indeed, contemporary "rights-talk" often resembles the scene in one of the *Star Trek* films where Captain Kirk and his cohorts are engaged in negotiations of some sort with the Klingons and the Chekhov character raises the issue of the Klingons' lack of regard for "democracy and human rights." A Klingon responds by denouncing the term "human rights" as "racist" (presumably because Klingons are excluded from the human rights pantheon).

Benoist traces the development of modern "human rights" ideology and explores how the concept of "rights" has changed throughout history. In the classical world, "rights" were conceived of as being relative to an individual's relationship to a particular community. Someone possessed "rights" because they were a citizen of a specific political entity or some other institutional context. The notion of abstract "rights" in a quasi-metaphysical sense was non-existent. Benoist considers the ideology of human rights to be an outgrowth of Christian universalism. Christianity introduced the concept of an individual soul that is eternal, transcendent, and independent of one's specific social identity. Out of the Christian notion of the transcendent soul emerged the Enlightenment doctrine of "natural rights." These rights are assumed to be universal and immutable.

Yet the very concept of "rights" as conceived of in this manner has itself undergone a number of profound metamorphosis. In its early phase, rights doctrine recognized only the Lockean negative liberties of "life, liberty, and property" and so forth. With the advent of ideologies like socialism or progressive liberalism the rights doctrine began to include what are now called "positive" rights. F. D. Roosevelt's famous "four freedoms" are an illustration of the foundations of this perspective. With the racial and cultural revolutions of the postwar era, rights doctrine took on a whole new meaning with "rights" now including exemption from discrimination on the basis of ethnicity, gender, sexual orientation, disability and an increasingly long list of other things. This certainly would have come as a shock to the great apostle of "natural rights," Thomas Jefferson, who, as the Left never ceases to remind us, was a white male slaveholder who thought homosexuals should be castrated.

The definition of "human rights" continues to become increasingly murky over time. Benoist provides an apt illustration of the escalating imprecision of the rights doctrine by citing this quote from Pierre Manent:

To respect the dignity of another human being is no longer to respect the respect which he conserves in himself for the moral law; it is today, more and more, to respect the choice that he has made, whatever this choice may be, in the realization of his rights.

Benoist describes the predictable outcome of the rights doctrine that is now observable in contemporary politics:

The present tendency...consists in converting all sorts of demands, desires, or interests into 'rights.' Individuals, in the extreme case, would have the 'right' to see no matter what demand satisfied, for the sole reason that they can formulate them. Today, to claim rights is only a way of seeking to maximize one's interests.

Particularly disastrous has been the fusion of the rights doctrine with mass democracy and the parallel growth exhibited by these two. Hans Hermann Hoppe has observed that a mass democracy comprised of an infinite number of interest groups making infinite rights claims is simply a form of low-intensity civil war. Likewise, Welf Herfurth has demonstrated how the very meaning of "democracy" has changed over time whereby earlier definitions of this concept, even in their modern liberal variations, have been abandoned and "democracy" has simply become a pseudonym for the limitless right to personal hedonism.

A paradoxical effect of the infinite expansion of the rights doctrine has been the simultaneously infinite growth of the state. Fustel de Coulanges described the political order of pre-modern Europe:

At the top of the hierarchy, the king was surrounded by his great vassals. Each of these vassals was himself surrounded by his own feudatories and he could not pronounce the least judgment without them...The king could neither make a new law, nor modify the existing laws, nor raise a new tax without the consent of the country...If one looks at the institutions of this regime from close quarters, and if one observes their meaning and significance, one will see they were all directed against despotism. However great the diversity that seems to reign in this regime, there is, however, one thing that unites them: this thing is obsession with absolute power. I do not think any regime better succeeded in rendering arbitrary rule impossible.

Benoist contrasts this with subsequent political developments in European civilization:

The end of the feudal regime marked the beginning of the disintegration of this system under the influence of Roman authoritarianism and the deadly blows of the centralized state. Little by little, hereditary royalty implemented a juridical-administrative centralization at the expense of intermediary bodies and regional assemblies. While the communal revolution sanctioned the power of the nascent bourgeoisie, the regional parliaments ceased to be equal assemblies and became meetings of royal officers. Having become absolute, the monarchy supported itself upon the bourgeoisie to liquidate the resistances of the nobility.

Indeed, it could be argued that a similar process is presently transpiring whereby the New Class (what Sam Francis called the "knowledge class" or what Scott Locklin regards as simply a new upper middle class) is aligning itself with the central government for the purpose of destroying the traditional WASP elite and marginalizing the traditional working to middle classes just as the nascent bourgeoisie of earlier times aligned itself with absolute monarchies against the nobility.

The growth of the rights doctrine has of course brought with it the explosive growth of rights-enforcement agencies and bureaucrats as any small business owner or self-employed person who has dealt with Occupational Health and Safety Administration would agree. Likewise, the autonomy of regions, localities, and the private sector has been nearly entirely eradicated in the name of creating rights for an ever expanding army of grievance groups and their advocates. Benoist discusses how the rights doctrine has also resulted in the phenomenal growth of the legal system. Today, there is virtually no aspect of life that is considered to be beyond the reach of state regulation or prohibition. Says Pierre Manent:

In the future, if one depends principally upon human rights to render justice, the 'manner of judging' will be irreparable. Arbitrariness, that is to say precisely what our regimes wanted to defend themselves against in instituting the authority of constitutionality, will then go on increasing, and will paradoxically become the work of judges. Now, a power which discovers that it can act arbitrarily will not delay in using and abusing this latitude. It tends towards despotism.

Far more dreadful than the use of "rights" as a pretext for enlarging civil bureaucracies and creeping statism in domestic and legal matters has been the application of the "human rights" ideology to international relations. Benoist points out the irony of how the military imperialism that the decolonization movements were ostensibly supposed to end has been revived under the guise of "humanitarian intervention." The doctrine of "humanitarian intervention" not only contravenes the international law established by the Peace of Westphalia but as well the Charter of the United Nations: *"It suggests that every state, whatever it be, can intervene at will in the internal affairs of another state, whatever it be, under the pretext of preventing 'attacks on human rights.'"* The effect of this doctrine is the simple sanctioning of aggressive war without end.

Plato's observation that a democratic regime on its deathbed is most typically characterized by a combination of individual licentiousness and creeping political tyranny would seem to be apt assessment of our present condition. As one Facebook commentator recently suggested:

> *Barbarism. Take a picture, we need to get it down for future civilizations. They need to know how the dialectic works: the negation of parental and local authority does NOT lead to freedom, or does so only briefly. That negation is in turn negated by a soft totalitarianism, now becoming harder and more crystallized in order to fill the vacuum of authority. If we record it for them, when some future Neo-Enlightenment philosopher promises liberty and equality circa 2800CE, he can be properly dressed down before he does any damage.*

Hear, hear!

8

Totalitarian Humanism and Mass Immigration

Speech delivered at the National Policy Institute Conference on
September 10, 2011 in Washington, D.C.

When Richard very graciously invited me to speak to this gathering, one of the first things I thought about was the fact that many people would no doubt wonder why someone with my political background and orientation would even be at a conference like this in the first place. Given that I am an anarchist, and this is a conference on nationalism, many would ask the question of whether anarchism and nationalism are not diametrically opposed perspectives. Certainly, the ardent critics of nationalism, whose ranks include many self-proclaimed anarchists, would likely feel this way and many who consider themselves nationalists might also consider the relationship between anarchism and nationalism to be an incompatible one.

I, for one, would deny the incompatibility of this relationship. I could cite the words of another anarchist who recently remarked that if you are opposed to one world government, you are already an anarchist of a kind, as you would then favor an anarchism of nations if not communities or individuals, and that the rest is just haggling over the details. So perhaps we are not as far apart on this question as we might think. However, my own reasons for holding to the views that I do involves a question that I think is much more substantive in nature and that is the question of what I call "totalitarian humanism."

Totalitarian Humanism is simply my term for what is more commonly called "political correctness." I did not coin this term. Instead, I picked it up from an anonymous, underground British writer some years ago, a writer whose real name I never knew. But I prefer the term "totalitarian humanism" because I think it is the one that best describes the worldview associated with political correctness. The essence of totalitarian humanism can be identified with an observation from Joseph de Maistre who said in observation of the political order that was to eventually arise out of the French Revolution (quote):

Totalitarian Humanism and Mass Immigration

The constitution of 1795, like its predecessors, has been drawn up for Man. Now, there is no such thing in the world as Man. In the course of my life, I have seen Frenchmen, Italians, Russians, etc.; I am even aware, thanks to Montesquieu, that one can be a Persian. But, as for Man, I declare that I have never met him in my life. If he exists, I certainly have no knowledge of him.

....This constitution is capable of being applied to all human communities from China to Geneva. But a constitution which is made for all nations is made for none: it is a pure abstraction, a school exercise whose purpose is to exercise the mind in accordance with a hypothetical ideal, and which ought to be addressed to Man, in the imaginary places which he inhabits....(end quote)

The worldview that I have characterized as totalitarian humanism is also the worldview that dominates all of our institutions in the modern Western world. It is the prevailing ideology of our political classes, our economic and business elite, and our cultural and intellectual elite. It is the worldview that is taught in our educational systems from the kindergarten level all the way up through the postgraduate level. Indeed, it seems as though the more education one has, the more likely it is that one has completely internalized this worldview. This is the worldview that dominates the mass media and entertainment industry which in our modern societies is a major force in the shaping of public opinion, perhaps comparable in many ways to the role of the Church during past eras in the history of Western civilization. In fact, this is the worldview that is preached in the pulpits of many contemporary Christian churches, and not just among the mainline liberal denominations but even among those with an ostensibly conservative theological orientation.

The ideology of totalitarian humanism insists that profound human differences regarding matters of culture, nationality, ethnicity, race, religion, or language are simply of no significance. Differences of these kinds that have been generated by thousands of years of human social evolution and have produced many magnificent variations of human culture that have existed since ancient times are dismissed by the proponents of totalitarian humanism as mere surface-level social constructs that contain no essence or intrinsic value. Some proponents of this worldview have gone even further and insisted that the variations to be found among human populations are merely interchangeable commodities. According to this kind of reasoning, if it can be called that, the differences between Western civilization or Islamic civilization or Chinese civilization are really no more important than the differences between MacDonald's or Pizza Hut or Kentucky Fried Chicken.

Some have objected to my use of the term "humanism" is this particular way. After all, were not the ancient Greeks who essentially founded our civilization also humanists? Was not the Renaissance, a defining era in the history of the evolution of Western civilization, also a humanistic project? Still others have mistakenly identified my criticisms of what I call "totalitarian humanism" as attacks on secularism. After all, was Nietzsche not an atheist along with Hobbes and Hume before him? As a consequence of this confusion, it is important to understand that I am not using the term "humanism" is the classical sense. Nor am I using the term as a synonym for secularism or atheism. Indeed, I count myself as something of a disciple of Nietzsche and I share many of his views regarding the impact of Christianity on Western civilization more generally. Instead, I am using the term "humanism" to describe a view of humanity, human nature and human civilizations whose core ideas are universalism, egalitarianism, and the linear-progressive view of history.

As I have already stated, the universalism implicit in the totalitarian humanist worldview denies the reality of innate and often profound differences which can be seen to exist among diverse human populations. This universalism is then followed by an incipient egalitarianism. If human differences are merely artificial or arbitrary social constructs with no intrinsic value, then inequalities found among human groups must also be unnatural, artificial, or arbitrary, according to this worldview.

It therefore follows, if one accepts this view, that inequality among human populations is the result of either a lack of effort on the part of humanity generally to eradicate inequality, or malevolence on the part of those who are seen to be the perpetrators of inequality. Another aspect of the totalitarian humanist worldview that I am describing that is not as frequently discussed but is in my view at least vital to understanding this worldview is the notion of a progressive view of history. According to such a view, history is perpetually moving towards higher levels of human progress in such a way that ordinary human foibles and failures will no longer be relevant. We see this worldview, for instance, in the Christian notion of the lamb lying down with the wolf. More relevant to our purposes here today, we see this worldview active in the bold proclamations of contemporary liberals and leftists, whose ranks include most so-called conservatives, and who insist that human conflicts of the kind that have existed since time immemorial over differences of culture, race, or nationality will disappear if only human beings can learn to live together in peace and harmony.

Given my own political identity, the totalitarian aspect of what I call "totalitarian humanism" is a matter that I am particularly concerned about. We are all familiar with the totalitarian political ideologies of the twentieth century and the consequences they brought about for mankind. These twentieth century totalitarian ideologies differed considerably among themselves concerning the specific nature of their ideals, but a common thread to be found among them is their deification of the state and their desire for the state to maintain an all-encompassing presence in the wider human society. I would submit that many of the proponents of the totalitarian humanist worldview at least implicitly share a similar vision of the state. While even some of our colleagues who are here today have had the experience of living under a totalitarian left-wing regime, most of us who originate from North America, Great Britain, Western Europe, or Australia have no such experiences in our own personal histories. Yet, as some thinkers of the European New Right and others have suggested, what we have seen emerge in our contemporary Western nations is a kind of "soft totalitarianism."

We may not yet be at the level of repression found in the Stalinist states, with their secret police, concentration camps, arbitrary arrests in the middle of the night, and psychiatric incarcerations. However, we can observe all around us efforts to repress and silence those who would speak critically of the worldview that presently dominates all of our institutions. The fact that this gathering itself is being held in a public facility under police protection as it would be imprudent for reasons we are all aware of to hold this conference in a private facility is by itself testimony of the creeping totalitarianism we find all around us today. In recent times, previous efforts to hold conferences with themes very similar to this one have been prevented either by the efforts of self-appointed vigilantes using threats of extra-legal violence while the state has looked the other way or by use of behind-the-scenes political pressure exercised by public officials. Such incidents are chilling examples of soft totalitarianism, or perhaps of what the late Sam Francis referred to as "anarcho-tyranny." Indeed, we here in the United States are actually fortunate that the First Amendment allows us to gather at all as a conference of this type might well be legally prohibited in some other Western nations.

The Tyranny of the Politically Correct

Some years ago, I wrote an article for the LewRockwell.Com website, which I believe is still available from that site's archives, where I outlined the relationship of totalitarian humanism to the state. Then as now, I maintained that the political vision implicit in the totalitarian humanist worldview is one where the all-pervasive presence of the state in human affairs is legitimized on an ideological level by the kind of utopian universalism, radical egalitarianism, and belief in an abstract conception of "progress" to which the adherents of totalitarian humanism subscribe. We see manifestations of this all around us as well. At the level of local government, we see the persistent efforts of state agencies ranging from the public school system to the child protective services to the family courts to undermine the sovereignty and integrity of institutions that are in competition with the state such as the family, religion, private associations, and the general community. At the level of the national government, we see attacks on the autonomy of the private sector, civil society, regions and localities in the name of advancing leftist-egalitarian ideals. Even in the realm of foreign policy and international relations, we see aggressive war being waged in the name of liberal presumptions such as the alleged universal sanctity of so-called "democracy."

I would likewise submit that mass immigration is the primary weapon being utilized by the proponents of the totalitarian humanist worldview. One of the great ironies of the situation with mass immigration is that it involves a de facto alliance between the forces of the radical cultural left on one hand and big business and super-capitalism on the other hand. The enthusiasm for mass immigration demonstrated by contemporary Western elites can, I believe, be understood on two different levels. The first of these involves matters of naked self-interest on the part of those who are proponents of mass immigration. A number of scholars who are also immigration skeptics have produced powerful critiques of the vast array of political interests that benefit from mass immigration. As previously mentioned, the capitalist elites or big business or whatever we wish to call it is one of these. In an article by Alain de Benoist that was posted on the Occidental Observer website, Benoist refers to mass immigration as the "reserve army of capital" and discusses the role of political agitation by big business elites in the implementation of de facto open borders immigration policies. Most of us are probably aware of the revelation by Tony Blair's former speechwriter Andrew Neather back in 2009 that the Labour regime of Mr. Blair deliberately pursued an open borders policy for the sake of making the U.K. more multicultural. In both of these instances, we see a cynical calculation on the part of either the business class in the former instance or the political class in the latter instance to utilize mass immigration for the sake of the short term advancement of their own economic or political self-interest without any regard whatsoever for the long term consequences of such immigration for the future of their nation or their posterity.

Mass immigration is supported by businessmen who want the cheap labor that immigrants provide, politicians who want their votes, ethnic lobbies who wish to increase their own numbers, public sector bureaucrats who wish to obtain more clients for their services thereby guaranteeing themselves job security, education professionals who wish to increase both the size of their student bodies and the size their budgets, and religious professionals who see immigrant populations as a possible source of replacements for their own dwindling congregations. Many other examples could be provided of those who cynically endorse open borders in the hope that mass immigration will advance their own narrow, immediate interests.

But there are also others who endorse mass immigration for reasons that transcend mere personal selfishness. There are those who consider support for mass immigration to be a matter of profound moral concern. It is these people who are the leading or at least most zealous proponents of the worldview that I have described as totalitarian humanism. According to the morality to which such people subscribe, Western civilization must atone for such past injustices as racism, imperialism, colonialism, Nazism, or the Holocaust by what amounts to the surrender of Western civilization itself to the invading Third World immigrant masses. That such a surrender would amount to the destruction of a civilization that has evolved over thousands of years and the dispossession of indigenous Europeans in their historic, ancestral homelands is of no concern to those who hold to this worldview. Indeed, they cheer on the advent of such destruction and dispossession as part of the march towards what they believe will be greater progress and greater equality. Just as the proponents of the worldview I have characterized as totalitarian humanism give no thought to the long term future survival of their civilization, so do they give no concern to the more immediately tangible and observable consequences of mass immigration. As the writer Derek Turner recently observed in an article for AlternativeRight.Com (quote):

> "Diversity" has such talismanic importance in America's public culture that almost everything else is hazarded to accommodate

its ever more outré demands social cohesion, the interests of the majority population, free speech, fiscal responsibility, political accountability, academic excellence, environmental protection, immigration control, government effectiveness, police effectiveness, military effectiveness and sometimes even in prisons, where staff refuse to segregate racial gangs. Even some conservatives now publicly defend "diversity," either out of ignorance of its effects or because to condemn it would mean acknowledging that America has been pursuing a woefully wrong-headed policy for decades, under Republican as much as Democrat administrations.

One thing that I have personally found to be the most interesting and perplexing about the unbridled support given to mass immigration from the political Left has been the Left's utter obliviousness regarding the incompatibility of such support with other ideals that the Left ostensibly holds to be sacred such as women's right, gay rights, secularism, legalized abortion, a lenient and humane penal system, the deregulation of private moral behavior, the promotion of alternative lifestyles, and so forth. Clearly, mass immigration is not in the interests of the domestic working classes or the domestic poor. And while mass immigration is certainly harmful to the interests of the historic white majority in the United States, it is arguably even more harmful to America's traditional minority groups such as blacks, American Indians, Mexican-Americans, or Asian-Americans. For instance, we are already observing the ethnic cleansing of African-American neighborhoods in southern California by Hispanic immigrant gangs. Nor is it immediately clear as to how the importation of mass numbers of Arabs, Muslims, and other Third World immigrants into the West serves the long term interests of the West's historic Jewish minority population.

I would submit here today that mass immigration is the most serious issue our civilization faces at present. Many other aspects of our current political and cultural situation can be corrected with time. Foolish laws such as those creating thought crimes in the name of combating "hate" or prohibiting free speech can be repealed. Anti-meritocratic policies such as affirmative action can be rescinded. Wrongheaded government programs can be abolished. The failings of particular institutions, whether they are governments or armies or universities or banks, can be corrected through changes in institutional leadership, or through the creation of newer and better institutions. But mass immigration is the one policy that, once it reaches a certain tipping point, cannot be undone. If mass immigration continues and even expands, eventually our civilization will reach the point of no return, and thousands of years of cultural evolution will be lost as a result of demographic overrun. There is no law of history that guarantees a civilization's perpetual survival. We know from the example of the classical Greco-Roman civilization of antiquity that even the greatest and most powerful civilizations can eventually become extinct. Let us not allow Western civilization to once again suffer such a fate. Thank you for listening to me.

9

American Imperialism vs.
The Identity of the World's Peoples

Speech delivered at the National Policy Institute on October 31, 2015.

I was very happy when I was asked to speak to this gathering on the topic of the conflict between American imperialism and European identity, and indeed the identity of virtually all of the world's peoples.

I have been an outspoken critic of American imperialism for several decades now, and as someone who has his political origins on the far Left, for much of that time I was mostly concerned about the relationship between the United States and the underdeveloped world. However, after spending some time in Europe off and on for the past fifteen years, I've also come to realize that much of the criticism that can be voiced concerning the relationship between the United States and the underdeveloped world is also quite applicable to the relationship between the United States and Europe.

I will explain why that is in a moment, but first let me say that I consider American imperialism to be the bastard child of European colonialism, and it was a child that grew up to be a monster that ended up eating its father. I will explain what I mean by that in a moment as well. But I also think a bit of historical perspective is necessary in order to fully understand this question.

Two hundred years ago, most of the peoples around the world were still in the hunter and gatherer stage in terms of their level of social evolution. This is something that most contemporary people have no awareness of. It's certainly something that my students are surprised to hear when I tell them about it. But during the thousands of years that civilization has existed, within the broader context of all of humanity, civilization has still been the exception rather than the rule, at least until very, very recently. While many of the criticisms of European colonialism that are frequently voiced are indeed quite legitimate in my view, it is also true that a major part of the legacy of European colonialism is that it brought the virtues of Western civilization to many other parts of the world. Now, I am not someone who thinks that white, Western civilization is all that there is and that everything else is garbage. That would be a totally ahistorical perspective, in my view. But I would argue that the legacy of European colonialism is comparable to the legacy of Alexander the Great, who brought the virtues of classical Greek civilization to what in the fourth century B.C. (or B.C.E. if we want to be PC about it, but I guess I don't need to worry about that here), but what in the fourth century B.C. was most of the known world.

When I say that American imperialism is the bastard child of European colonialism, what I mean by that is that on one hand America is very much a product of European colonialism. We Americans did get our start as British colonies, as we know. However, it is also true that during the middle part of the twentieth century, the Europeans happened to engage in a particularly fratricidal war, which was probably the most tragic episode in world history, and one of the long terms results of this war was that the old European colonial empires essentially came to an end because their European mother countries had largely been laid to waste during the course of the war.

Now, I have a longstanding debate with a number of friends who are conservatives in the American sense, that is, loyal Republicans who can't get enough of FOX News, we all know the kinds of folks I'm talking about, the kind of people who think that the America of the 1950s was the apex of human civilization. These mainstream conservative types are often a bit bewildered when I explain to them that the reason America achieved what amounted to world dominance in the postwar era is because all of its competitors had been wiped out in the war. All that was left was Communism, which was a severe aberration, and the Third World which was largely mired in a pre-industrial state. With economic and geopolitical competitors of that type, of course the United States achieved world dominance. And, in fact, the United States stepped in and essentially picked up where the older European colonial empires left off. During the Cold War period, many of the former European colonies in Asia and Africa became American clients, and along with the American puppet states in Latin America, which represented the United States' traditional sphere of hegemony, all of these nations collectively became outposts of the American empire.

However, I would argue that American imperialism is different in character from European colonialism. European colonialism, in my view, was very much comparable to the old Roman empire of antiquity. The Roman Empire was certainly interested in exercising political, military, and economic hegemony over their subject peoples. However, the Roman Empire normally allowed its subject peoples to retain their own local cultures, traditions, religions, and ethnic identities. The Romans were mostly just concerned with collecting taxes and preventing rebellions, and not trying to transform their subject peoples in a fundamental way. Now, the subjects of the empire were expected to participate in the state cult of the emperor, but for most of the peoples of the Roman Empire this was not a problem since they were polytheists anyway. In fact, that's what got the Christians into so much trouble with the Roman authorities. As monotheists, they could have only one god. The Jews were actually exempt from participation in the state cult, by the way, but the Romans refused to extend that privilege to the Christians as well. I guess they figured once was enough.

But as far as the difference between American imperialism and European colonialism is concerned, I think something I observed the first time I ever went to Europe illustrates this dichotomy quite well. When I first ventured to Europe, one of the first things that I noticed was how old everything was: the architecture, the designs of the streets and the sidewalks, the public buildings, the art, the museums. Yet everywhere in the midst of this very old European cultural experience, I saw signs of Americanization. I recall, for example, observing scenery where these very old cathedrals would be intermixed with signs advertising American fast food restaurants, like McDonald's, or Burger King, or Kentucky Fried Chicken. As an American this was no big deal to me personally because I was already used to seeing this crass commercialism everywhere I went, but I recall thinking at the time that if I were a European I would be extremely offended by this form of cultural imperialism that was all around.

I think this experience illustrates very well a crucial difference between American imperialism and more traditional forms of imperialism or colonialism. American imperialism has a quasi-religious quality to it in the sense that it is not just about to whom taxes get paid, but instead it is about changing the way that people live in a much wider sense, changing the way they think, and altering their identity in very fundamental ways. And I think this is true of American imperialism as it pertains to Europe as much as it pertains to other parts of the world. But we see examples of this everywhere. A friend of mine, a national-anarchist by the name of Welf Herfurth, tells the story of visiting Saigon in Vietnam, supposedly a Communist nation, and observing Vietnamese youngsters on the streets of Saigon trying to emulate the mannerisms of American rap singers. Today in Japan, for the first time ever, the Japanese are starting to have a problem with obesity. Now, when we think of the Japanese we normally don't think about fat people. We think of healthy people who have traditionally enjoyed comparative long life expectancies because of their healthy diets of fish and rice. However, due to the importation of American fast food culture into Japan, the Japanese are now starting to experience problems with obesity and the health difficulties that result from this.

American imperialism is not merely about exercising political hegemony, it is about facilitating what is thought to be a moral transformation of other peoples and cultures. And as I said, I believe there is a quasi religious mentality associated with this kind of moral crusading. One thing that is distinctive about Christianity is that it teaches that temptation is just as great a sin as acting on temptation. For example, Christianity teaches that hating someone is as great a moral failure as murdering them, or that desiring another man's wife is the same as actually adulterating the wife of another. Most ethical or religious philosophies teach that the essence of virtue is the process of overcoming temptation or refusing to give in to temptation, not that merely experiencing temptation and succumbing to temptation are one and the same. I believe that the morality that drives the ideology of the contemporary Western world is a secularization of this kind of traditional Christian blurring of the distinction between thoughts and actual deeds. For example, it has always seemed to me that the real problem that liberals and leftists have with racism, or homophobia, or patriarchy, or whatever Ism or Archy or Phobia happens to be on the chopping block this week, is not necessarily any tangible or identifiable harms that are associated with these as much as the mere idea that someone, somewhere, somehow might think racist or homophobic thoughts. It is the impurity of their hearts and not the malevolence of their deeds that is somehow the real problem. The greatest fear of the Left is that someone might be hiding away in a broom closet thinking about racism.

This is the morality that I also believe guides the American Empire. In fact, when the Islamists refer to American imperialists as the modern Crusaders, I think they have a point, not necessarily in the way they mean it, but it is an apt analogy. As an illustration, in a speech delivered in Chicago in June of 2014, Hillary Clinton suggested that if she were to become President of the United States that feminist ideology would be a central component part of her approach to foreign policy, and we can only imagine where that will eventually lead. Earlier this year, we observed the spectacle of President Obama traveling to Kenya in order to lecture their president on gay rights. And, of course, we remember the uproar a few years ago when a number of political forces in the Western world were calling for a boycott of the 2014 Winter Olympics in Russia over Russia's failure to, I don't know, endorse gay marriage or whatever the problem was. In 1980, the United States under President Carter boycotted the Olympics in Moscow because of the Soviet Union's invasion of the sovereign state of Afghanistan. Less than thirty-five years later, we saw Americans and others calling for a boycott of the Olympics in Russia in the name of gay rights, which I suppose says a great deal about the direction that the Western world has gone in during the past third of a century.

And we see that this liberal crusader mentality has produced disaster all over the world.

Recall, for example, the so-called "Freedom Agenda" of the former Bush administration, and that was part of the ideological rationale for the war in Iraq. I suppose we can gauge how well that worked out by observing what a paradise Iraq is today. Remember the military action against Libya in 2011, led by the Obama administration, and ostensibly under the pretext of defending human rights, which led to the creation of the failed state that Libya is today. Recall the so-called "Arab Spring" and the efforts of the United States to undermine secular governments in Arab nations, in the name of spreading democracy, which is supposedly something that all people everywhere want, irrespective of their history, culture, or traditions, I guess because Francis Fukuyama told us so, or whatever. But the real impact of the "Arab Spring," as Mr. Putin recently pointed out, was the coming to power of Islamists in some countries and the growth of terrorist organizations in others. So we are able to plainly see that all of this crusading for democracy and human rights has actually led to a reduction of democracy and human rights, or at least a reduction in humans.

Now, aside from the loss of blood and treasure that has been generated by American military imperialism, we are also able to observe the loss of identity that is taking place because of American economic and cultural imperialism. In nation after nation around the world, American television, popular music, popular culture, fashion, media, fast food, and consumer culture are increasingly everywhere. It's as if the ambition is for the entire planet to become one giant, universal Wal-Mart. And what is happening is that the unique identities of people all over the world are being eradicated.

There are essentially three kinds of identity that are acceptable according to the value system on which American imperialism is implicitly based. One of these is the identity of a subject to state. Notice that I didn't say "citizen." I said "subject." There is the identity of the worker or the professional, whereby someone's identity comes to be defined by their place in the economy. And there is the identity of the consumer, the role of the individual as a participant in the marketplace. No other form of identity is acceptable within the context of this particular paradigm. Not ethnicity, not nationality, not race, not culture, not religion, not history, not tradition, not community, not ancestry, not family, and apparently, not even gender. Instead, the ambition is to create masses of helots that function merely as deracinated, working, consuming, tax-paying, obedient drones without any connection to the past, no regard for the future, no folklore, no distinctiveness, and no serious aspirations. That is the vision that is implicit in the rhetoric and in the practice of the American Empire.

Now, the question that emerges from this critique of the American Empire and its impact on the identities of the world's peoples is the matter of how to go about building resistance. This question in turn raises some very fundamental geopolitical questions. I have a generally optimistic view because already we see significant pockets of resistance developing all over the world. I interpret present day international relations largely in terms of what I call "Team A" versus "Team B." Team A is the dominant coalition with the framework of the international power elite, or the international plutocracy, or international capitalism, or whatever you want call it. This dominant coalition is what I call the Anglo-American-Zionist-Wahhabist axis consisting of the United States as the senior partner, along with England, Israel, Saudi Arabia, the other Gulf States, and most of the member states of NATO and the European Union as junior partners.

As far as the present day relationship between Europe and the United States is concerned, I'm inclined to think that it was ironically Mao Zedong who had the best analysis of that. In the early 70s, Maoist China developed what they called the "Three Worlds Theory," which is not the same thing as the idea of the First, Second, and Third World that you found in Western political theory during the same period.

Instead, the Maoist model argued that the world order of the time consisted of the First World, which was the United States and its satellites, including Western Europe, the Second World, which was the Soviet Union and its satellites, and the Third World of what they considered to be exploited nations. And I would suggest that a modified version of this theory is still applicable, with the modification being that the Second World has disappeared, and that most of the former Soviet satellites have become American satellites with Russia losing its superpower status.

And out of this situation is emerging what I call Team B. The foundation of Team B is what I refer as the triangular resistance, that is, three distinctive blocks of nations that are emerging in opposition to American imperialism. The most significant of these is the emergence of the so-called BRICS, that is, the economic alliance of Brazil, Russia, India, China, and South Africa. There is also what is called the Resistance Block in the Middle East, which consists of Iran, Syria, Hezbollah, a variety of Iraqi and Palestinian groups, the Houthi in Yemen. The third pattern of resistance consists of what I call "resistance nations" or resistance movements in Latin America that resist their own incorporation into the American Empire. This block also includes Brazil, Venezuela, Cuba, Ecuador, Bolivia, and Argentina with varying degrees of consistency, as well as the wider set of Latin American populist movements that these nations to some degree represent. In addition to these three blocks of resistance, there are also outliers like Belarus, North Korea, Zimbabwe, and the Kurdish independence movement that has recently emerged. There are also a variety of non-state actors around the world reflecting a wide range of identities that are resistant to incorporation into the American empire and its program of global liberal capitalist imperialism. So resistance is building everywhere even as the weaknesses of the American empire become increasingly obvious.

In particular, Russia, China, and Iran have emerged as bulwarks against U.S. imperialism, and we have in recent times seen a greater cooperation between these nations, for example, in the currency swap agreement between Russia and China, or the collaboration between Russia and Iran in the war against ISIS, and I have seen discussion recently concerning the possibility of Iran joining the BRICS alliance.

Ultimately, however, we also need an independent and self-assertive Europe. If I could give any advice to the European nations it would be to break out from underneath the American Empire, dissolve NATO, and claim self-determination for themselves and this includes military self-determination as well as political, economic, and cultural self-determination. The United States is on its way to becoming a failed state, with a $19 trillion national debt, the largest national debt in world history, and a society where virtually all of its institutions are increasingly dysfunctional. This is not system that will go on forever. Those of us who are Americans should be preparing ourselves for a post-America. Meanwhile, the Europeans should, in my view, strive to reclaim their own heritage and destiny. Ultimately, however, the salvation of Europe is dependent upon the abolition of the American Empire.

Thank you for listening to me.

10

The Fruits of Anarchist "Anti-Racism"

Certain attitudes derived from the New Left and the so-called counter-culture permeated neo-anarchism and had a deleterious effect upon it. Chief among these was elitism. It was the common belief among the New Left that the majority of the population was "co-opted", "sold-out," "racist" and "sexist." For the hippie-left, most people were considered to be beer-swilling, short-haired rednecks. Much of this youthful hostility was directed against their parents and hence was more of an expression of adolescent rebellion than political insight. With the exception of those who opted for anarcho-syndicalism, most neo-anarchists carried this contemptuous attitude with them. The majority was written-off as hopelessly corrupted and this attitude still continues today. Such contempt is in complete contrast to classical anarchism, which even at its most vanguardist, saw itself as only a catalyst or spokesman for the masses. While rejecting the majority, they became infatuated with minorities. The New Left, scorning workers, turned to racial minorities and the "poor" as possible agents of social change. Native people, prisoners, drop-outs, homosexuals, all have been given a high profile, virtually to the exclusion of the rest of the population." - Larry Gambone, *Sane Anarchy*, 1995

A recent article in the *Intelligence Report*, the journal of the state-connected, crony-capitalist, cop-friendly, "private" espionage and surveillance agency known the Southern Poverty Law Center remarked:

> *"Unifying anarchists has been likened to herding cats. But if there is one theme that most anarchists will rally around, it is that of stamping out racism, especially organized racism driven by white nationalist ideology. Many younger anarchists are members of Anti-Racist Action, a national coalition of direct-action "antifa" (short for "anti-fascist") groups that confront neo-Nazis and racist skinheads in the street, often resulting in violence."*

And what do these anarchists have to show for all of this "anti-racist" zealotry? How well are these anarchists regarded by actually existing people of color for their efforts? An item that has recently been circulating in the anarchist milieu with the revealing title, "Smack a White Boy, Round Two," demonstrates just how much "solidarity" is felt towards the mostly, white, middle-class, left-anarchist movement by the supposed beneficiaries of its anti-racism:

> Dread locked white punks, crusties with their scabies friends, and traveling college bros swarmed a space on the dividing line of gentrification in the Bloomfield/Garfield/Friendship area late July 2009 in Pittsburgh for the annual CrimethInc convergence. Whereas previous CrimethInc. convergences had been located deep in wooded areas, this particular one took place in a poor, black neighborhood that is being pushed to the borders by entering white progressive forces.

> There were those that had experienced CrimethInc's oppressive culture and people for years and others who had experienced enough oppression after just a few days. Our goals were to stop CrimethInc, their gentrifying force, and to end the convergence right then and there for all that they had done.

> Just a few blocks away, eight anarchist/autonomous/anti-authoritarian people of color* gathered to discuss a direct confrontation. We arrived from different parts of these stolen lands of the Turtle Island. Some came from the Midwest, some from the Northeast, some born and raised in Pittsburgh. Altogether we represented 7 different locations, half of us socialized as female a variety of sizes, skin color, with identities of queers, trans, gender-queers, gender variants, and womyn. With little time and a desire for full consensus, we quickly devised a plan.

> The majority of the CrimethInc kids were in the ballroom on the second floor watching and participating in a cabaret. A group of us began gathering attendees' packs, bags, shoes, banjos, and such from the other rooms on the second floor and moving it all down the hallway towards the stairs. We had gone pretty unnoticed, mostly due to lack of lighting.

> Once those rooms had been emptied, it was time for the main event. We gathered at the ballroom's doorway furthest from the stairs following the final act of the cabaret.

The Tyranny of the Politically Correct

"On the count of three. One, two, three!" one APOCista said.

"Get the fuck out!", we all shouted.

And the eviction began. One apocer began reading 'An Open Letter to White Radicals/Progressives', while the others began yelling at the attendees to gather their things and leave. Irritated by their continued inaction after about 10 minutes or so, one of the people involved in the action shouted, "This is not an act! Get your shit, or we'll remove it for you!"

So much for the claims of anarchists to be exemplars of multicultural brotherly love. Now, before I get to other questions, let me say that I actually think the "Anarchist People of Color" group who carried out this "eviction" had a point. Many white leftists and progressives do indeed regard non-whites as children in need of rescue by enlightened folks such as themselves, and often assume a paternalistic attitude when dealing with people of color. And while I'm not so sure that "gentrification" by white anarchist kids is quite on the level of gentrification by upper-middle class, affluent, professional people organized into state-connected "civic organizations" and "business associations", and operating in collusion with crony-capitalist "developers", the overall point is still well-taken. Gentrification does indeed frequently assume the character of a kind of urban imperialism, and white, middle-class "progressives" who never tire of wearing their racial liberalism on their sleeves are often at the forefront of such efforts. Indeed, it might be argued that gentrification serves the same purpose in modern urban societies as the dispossession of native or indigenous peoples' in frontier or colonial societies, i.e., naked robbery carried out under the banner of enlightenment, progress, paternalism or cultural and class chauvinism. Some would go even further and argue that mass immigration serves a similar purpose, e.g., economic and cultural dispossession of the indigenous poor and working class in order to provide labor for capitalists, clients for social services bureaucrats and voters for political parties and ethnic lobbies. But that might be "racism".

The obsession with "racism" exhibited by modern leftists appears to be rooted in a number of things. Some are the obvious, e.g., the political, cultural and intellectual backlash against such horrors as Nazism, South African apartheid, "Jim Crow" in the American South, the Vietnam War and other manifestations of extreme colonialism. Another is the need for the radical Left to find a new cause once the horrors of Communism were revealed. Still another is the universalist ethos that emerged from Enlightenment rationalism. Yet another is the adolescent rebellion against society mentioned by Gambone. And another is the quasi-Christian moralism exhibited by many left-wingers: "Love thy exotically colored neighbor."

It's like this, my fellow anarchist comrades: World War Two is over. Hitler is dead. George Wallace is dead. Bull Connor is dead. Jim Crow has been relegated into the dustbin of history. Apartheid is finished, and Nelson Mandela eventually became South Africa's head of state. In case you haven't been paying attention, the United States now has a black President. Many of the largest American cities have black-dominated governments. In the wider society, "racism" has become the ultimate sin, much like communism or homosexuality might have been in the 1950s. By continuing to beat the dead horse of "white supremacy", anarchists are simply making our movement look like fools.

No doubt many reading this will raise issues such as the high rates of imprisonment among blacks and Hispanics, police brutality, medical neglect of illegal immigrants in detention centers, or the high unemployment rates in American inner cities. Do you really think that no whites have ever been adversely affected by these things? Do you think there are no whites in jail or prison for frivolous reasons? Who receive shoddy medical care? Who are adversely affected by state-capitalism and plutocratic rule? Who are subject to police harassment or violence, or who are shabbily treated by agents or bureaucrats of the state? Who are subject to social ostracism because of their class, culture, religion or lifestyle?

There is certainly nothing wrong with opposing the genuine oppression of people of other races or colors, and many anarchists and other radicals engage in laudable displays of support for the people of Palestine, Iraq, Afghanistan, Tibet, Latin America, and indigenous ethnic groups who are subjected to occupation or imperialist aggression. Yet, the obsession with "racism" found among many Western radicals has become pathological in nature. Whenever I encounter these "anti-racism" hysterics, I am reminded of the cultic, fundamentalist religious sects, where no amount of devotion to the cause is ever good enough. Go to church three times a week? Not good enough, you need to be there six times a week. And there is little doubt that the war between Anarchist People of Color and Crimethinc will produce a great deal of "What are we doing wrong, us shitty white supremacists?" self-flagellation among many "anti-racist" left-anarchists.

This obsession with "racism" on the part of many anarchists might be worth it if it had the effect of recruiting or converting many thousands or millions of people of color to our cause. Yet, the simple truth is that decades of anti-racism hysteria has produced an anarchist movement that is as white as it ever was. This does not mean that there are never any non-whites to be found in anarchist circles. Of course there are. But are they representative of the cultural norms of the ethnic or racial groups from where they came? Not in my experience. Instead, the relatively small numbers of people of color who can be found in North American anarchist circles are usually immigrants from other places, or products of ethnic minority cultures that have assimilated into a wider white culture, for instance, blacks who grew up in white middle-class neighborhoods or minorities who participate in white youth subcultures, like punk rock. Honestly speaking, what would a typical African-American or Latino think if they wandered into the standard anarchist discussion group and found themselves in the midst of the usual anarchist banter about "racism"? What would they think, other than, "What a bunch of freaks!"

This does not mean that anarchists should become "pro-racist". It simply means that it would be more productive if anarchists would simply re-orient themselves towards the ostensible purpose of anarchism, i.e., *"a political philosophy encompassing theories and attitudes which consider the state, as compulsory government, to be unnecessary, harmful, and/or undesirable, and promote the elimination of the state or anarchy."* I recently came across a Facebook page with the heading "The Other Anarchists" which described itself thus: *"For those who wish to see the state abolished, but are not nihilists, terrorists, or idiots. Including some: free market anti-capitalists, anarcho-capitalists, anarcho-monarchists, voluntaryists, social anarchists, Christian anarchists, Green anarchists, and our fellow travelers ([non-violent] Luddites, paleoconservatives, minarchists, left-conservatives, retroprogressives, and the like)."* This would seem to be about right. Perhaps we can work with the nihilists and terrorists, but the idiots really need to be shown the door. What should anarchists do about "racism"? *Just forget about it.* Many anarchists engage in many worthwhile projects that many different kinds of people can benefit from, like antiwar activism, labor solidarity, prisoner defense, support for the homeless, resisting police brutality, protecting animals from cruelty, environmental preservation, alternative media or alternative education. These are issues that transcend color lines. Just stick to these and let "people of color" work out their own problems for themselves.

The APOC/Crimethinc battle may well be indicative of what the future of the political Left will be. I have predicted before that the center-left will be dominant in American politics for the next several decades due to demographic, cultural and generational change in U.S. society. It is widely predicted that the non-white populations will collectively outnumber whites in the U.S. by the 2040s. As the non-white population grows due to demographic trends and large-scale immigration, and as class divisions widen, there is likely to be a split within liberalism between the mostly white, upper middle class, cultural progressives and the mostly black and Hispanic lower classes, which include many persons with more conservative views on social questions like gender roles, abortion, homosexuality and religion.

A Zogby poll taken last year concerning the level of public sympathy for the matter of secession indicated that the principal source of support for genuinely radical ideas (like separatism) comes not from the "far right" or backwoods militiamen but from young, unemployed, uneducated blacks and Hispanics in the heavily populated areas of the U.S.. In a few decades, the crumbling U.S. empire and its liberal-capitalist-multicultural elites and affluent classes may well be facing an insurgency by the expanded non-white underclass. There are an estimated one million urban gang members in the U.S., mostly blacks and Hispanics, and these are organized into thousands of armed groups. Are these not a domestic American version of the "fourth generation" insurgent movements that exist in other parts of the world like Latin America or the Middle East?

What will be the condition of American society in the decades ahead as the liberal-capitalist-multicultural ruling class begins to lose its grip and is faced with an insurgency by the black and Hispanic underclass? What should be the response of the mostly white anarchist movement to such a turn of events? How should the anarchist movement seek to handle such a scenario? Play your cards wrong and you'll end up in a situation infinitely worse than that faced by Crimethinc.

The anarchist milieu needs to re-think its positions concerning racial matters. Continuing to perpetrate anti-racism hysteria year after year, decade after decade is a dead end. There is zero evidence that such a stance will bring the masses of North American blacks and Hispanics

88

into our ranks, and much compelling evidence that such efforts are futile, foolish and counterproductive. For many years, the anarchist movement's obsession with "social issues" has been a distraction from what ought to be the primary objective of anarchism, i.e., the abolition of the state. This is not to say that anti-statism is the only value, or that anarchists should not be concerned with other matters. It does mean that a more constructive stance on certain questions should be pursued.

For one thing, it might be helpful if anarchists would display an interest in issues other than run of the mill left-wing causes like those involving race, gender, sexual orientation, ecology and the like. Why are anarchists not involved in the movement for the defense of the right to keep and bear arms? In a sensible anarchist movement, there would be anarchists sitting on the board of directors of the National Rifle Association. Why are anarchists not involved in the various movements for local or regional autonomy, or secession by states and communities? Certainly, such efforts should fit well with the supposed anarchist emphasis on decentralization.

What might be a more sensible approach to racial and cultural differences than the hysterical approach currently taken? A venerable American tradition is one of "separation of church and state." This is a tradition that has worked quite well throughout U.S. history. Individual Americans are largely free to practice or not practice whatever religion they wish. Yes, fringe religious groups like the Branch Davidians are sometimes subject to persecution. Yes, state laws such as the ban on the use of psychedelic drugs impedes powerless groups like certain indigenous tribes from practicing their religion. Yes, children from sects whose tenants prohibit certain medical practices are sometimes forcibly subjected to such practices. Yes, religious do-gooders sometimes wish to use the force of the laws to suppress activities deemed immoral, like gambling, vice or alcohol. But for the most part, most people practice their religion or non-religion of choice most of the time with very little interference from either the state, or from society at-large. Compare this with the situation in, say, Saudi Arabia or North Korea, and it can be determined that "separation of church and state" is a system that works quite well. Research shows, for instance, that atheists are a minority group that is more widely disliked than any of the groups championed by the Left: blacks, immigrants, homosexuals, Muslims. Yet atheists, of whom I am one, are hardly an "oppressed minority" but an intellectually and culturally elite group who are heavily represented within the ranks of leading scientists, philosophers, academics, journalists, authors, artists and entertainers. As far back as 1910, Thomas Edison was able to proclaim his heretical religious views with to the *New York Times* with impunity.

I submit that the appropriate attitude for anarchists to take concerning racial and cultural matters is one of "separation of race and state" or "separation of culture and state." Within such a context, all state legislation or regulation concerning race and culture would be eliminated, and individuals and groups would be able to engage in whatever racial or cultural practices they wished within the context of their own voluntary associations. Just as some religious organizations or institutions are very conservative or exclusionary in nature, and others are very liberal and inclusive, so might some racial or cultural organizations and institutions be similarly conservative or liberal, exclusionary or inclusive. For instance, the Anarchist People of Color and other like-minded groups could have their own schools, communities, neighborhoods, commercial enterprises and other institutions where white folks are verboten. Likewise, the Nation of Islam, Aztlan Nation, evangelical Christians, Mormons, paleoconservatives, or "national-anarchists" might also have their own homogenous communities as well. Feminists and queers might implement similar arrangements for themselves.

As I have said before, we need a "revolution within anarchism itself". We need an anarchist movement that is not just an all-purposes leftist movement, but a movement that has abolition of the state as its central focus, and an approach to matters of race, culture, religion and so forth that is workable in a highly diverse society. This renovated anarchist movement would shift its focus towards the building of autonomous, voluntary communities, reflecting a wide assortment of cultural, economic or ideological themes, within the context of a wider pan-separatist ethos whos principle enemy is the overarching state. It should be understood that severe and irreconcilable differences among different kinds of people will inevitably arise, and that such differences are best managed according to the principle of "peace through separatism." As Erik von Kuehnelt-Leddihn observed, "The ideological and philosophical struggles, which can neither be suppressed nor made an organic part of the governmental machine, have to be relegated to the private sphere of society."

11

Balkanization and the State of Exception

Keith Preston writes the blog Attack the System, which attempts to tie together both left and right anarchism in a Pan-secessionism against the empire.   While I come from a radically different perspective than Keith, I find his critique of the way many left anarchists are militant shock troops of liberalism to be a serious and disturbing critique as well as the Nietzschean critique of modernity to be taken seriously and not softened as it has been in French post-structuralism.

Skepoet: You started out in the libertarian socialist tradition but have moved towards a pan-anarchist movement than includes decentralized nationalists and non-socialists.   Could you describe how you left "left" anarchism in its socialist variety?

Keith Preston: I never really renounced "socialist-anarchism." I'm still interested in schools of thought that fall under that banner like syndicalism and mutualism, and I still very much consider the founding fathers (and mothers!) of classical anarchism to be influences on my thought. But I did abandon the mainstream (if it could be called that) of the socialist-anarchist movement. The reason for that is the left-anarchist milieu in its modern form is simply a youth subculture more interested in lifestyle issues (like veganism and punk music) than in revolutionary politics. And to the degree that these anarchists have any serious political perspective at all, it's simply a regurgitation of fairly clichéd left-progressive doctrines.

If one listens to what the mainstream anarchists talk about gay rights, global warming, immigrants rights, feminism, anti-racism, animal rights, defending the welfare state, the whole laundry list - they don't sound much different than what you would hear in the local liberal church parish, or at a Democratic party precinct meeting, or a university humanities course. Eventually, I came to the realization that a serious anti-state movement would need to be grounded in population groups whose core values really do put them at odds with the mainstream political culture. There are plenty of these: the urban underclass and underworld, religious sects whose exotic beliefs get them in trouble with the state, ethnic separatists, pro-gun militias, radical survivalists, drug cultures and sex cultures that are considered deviant or criminal, etc. I've been very happy to witness the growth of the anti-civilization movement within the ranks anarchism. What you label "decentralized nationalists" and non-socialists who oppose the state also fall into this category. So it's not so much about abandoning what I was before as much as building on that and expanding my perspective a bit.

S: Well, these movements have been around since the middle 1990s on my radar, but I have noticed that Occupy movement seems to have pushed these tensions back into the radical milieu, so to speak. What have you noticed in the past year on the ground?

K.P.: I consider Occupy Wall Street to largely be a recycling of the anti-globalization movement of the late 1990s and early 2000s. I am skeptical as to whether it will fare any better than the anti-globalization movement did. From what I have observed thus far, OWS is a fairly standard representation of the left-wing subculture, in the sense that the OWS movement seems to roll out a hodge-podge of relatively conventional left-of-center issues in a very chaotic way that lacks direction or vision. OWS is a movement that is easily ignored or co-opted by the establishment because it is does not threaten the system in any particularly significant way.

I essentially see OWS as the left's counterpart to the Teabaggers who were easily co-opted by the neocons. Where are the Teabaggers today? It will be fairly easy for the Democrats to co-opt OWS over the long haul. Look how easily the New Left of the 1960s was co-opted and that was a far more radical movement than OWS. The problem is that OWS offers no radical vision that is fundamentally at odds with the survival of the system. OWS has not developed a position of what might be called "radical otherness" in regards to its relationship to the political establishment.

I should probably add to my answer to your first question that I still very much consider socialist-anarchism of the leftist variety to be a legitimate part of the anarchist paradigm. My criticisms of that milieu are based on my perspective that it is too narrowly focused and that it is ineffective at actually attacking the state. The number of strands of anti-state, libertarian, or anti-authoritarian radicalism is quite numerous. I consider all of these, from anarcha-feminism to Islamic anarchism to queer anarchism to national-anarchism, to be different denominations of the broader anarchist philosophy, just like the Christian religion have its different denominational or sectarian variations. The problem I have with the left-anarchists is that I regard them as playing the same role in anarchism that a form of sectarian fundamentalism might play in Christianity. I wish to embrace all of the different tribes of the anarchist paradigm as brothers and sisters within the anarchist "faith," if you will, despite our own tribal, sectarian, or denominational differences and however much the different types of anarchists may hate each other.

My goal is for a civilization to emerge eventually where anarchism becomes the prevailing political, social, and economic philosophy, just as Christianity dominated medieval European civilization, Islam dominates the civilization of the Middle East, or Confucianism dominates traditional Chinese civilization.

I try to approach controversial social, political, or economic questions from an objective, scholarly perspective and I try to understand all different sides of issues and glean what tangible facts are available rather than simply relying on the established left-liberal paradigm that dominates the academic world as most anarchists seem to do. This ultimately leads to me taking a lot of unorthodox positions, although my primary concern is the area of anarchist strategy. I think philosophical abstractions are worthless if they can't be transmitted into real life action. I'm interested in questions like what should the priorities of anarchists be, given our current political conditions? What should be our principal goals? What are some real world goals we can set for ourselves that are actually achievable? What is the most practical approach to the question of what a civilization where the anarchist paradigm is the prevalent paradigm might look like? What are the answers questions of that nature?

S: It has been interesting to see your post-left readings of Carl Schmitt who is a jurist whose work was ignored for a long time and I think re-popularized primarily by the works of the left-wing philosophy Agamben and by thinkers on the European New Right. How is an anarchist like you informed by Schmitt?

K.P.: Schmitt's thought really unmasks the essence of the state in a way that I think is more penetrating than much anarchist thought because it lacks the ideological predisposition towards attacking the state that an anarchist would obviously have and there's also a lot of moral pretentiousness found in much anarchist writing. Schmitt is writing from the perspective of a brutally honest realist. He is one of those rare political theorists like Machiavelli, Hobbes, or Nietzsche who is able to analyze politics without much illusion.

Schmitt considered the true nature of the political to be organized collectives with the potential to engage in lethal conflict with one another. His concept of political sovereignty is also quite penetrating. As Schmitt said: "Sovereign is he who decides on the state of the exception." What he meant by that is that the real power in any society resides in those who are able to set aside the formal rule-making process and codified system of laws when it suits the interests of the state. The law is intended for subjects rather than rulers. The state is a ruler or collection of rulers who act in their own interests. The law serves to restrain subjects, and not to restrain rulers in any authentic sense. Within the realm of the truly political, rulers engage in perpetual brawling with other rulers or potential rulers.

S.: The sovereign exception is an interesting issue. So what is the anarchist answer to the idea of the sovereign exception?

K.P.: I think that in a civilization where anarchism was the prevailing political perspective the sovereign would be non-state entities that were capable of repelling physical threats to the anarchist polities. For instance, there might be anarchist-led militias, citizen posses, or private defense forces that would serve the function of resisting either an external invasion or the attempted seizure of power by any one political faction for the purpose of creating a new state.

This one reason why I think fourth generation warfare theory is so interesting because it postulates that the sovereignty of the state is receding and giving way to non-state actors in the realm of military conflict.

There are some interesting historical examples of sovereignty without the state. The Icelandic Commonwealth existed for several centuries minus a single sovereign entity with a monopoly on coercion. During the Spanish Civil War, the anarchist militia confederations essentially replaced the state in certain regions of Spain. An interesting contemporary example is Hezbollah, which has for the most part replaced the Lebanese state as the sovereign in Lebanese society. Of course, Hezbollah are not anarchists, but they are an illustration of how a sovereign can emerge that eclipses the state.

The Tyranny of the Politically Correct

S.: On the Fourth generation warfare: This seems to be used as an excuse to strengthen the state. Do you see this is a trend that is, at root, a sign that there are elements of the larger culture that are separating and going into radically different directions?

K.P.: Sure. I think a major part of the premise behind the US's "war on terrorism" is awareness on the parts of the overlords of the empire that the fourth generation resistance is rising and challenging the state in many different areas. So the state is trying to strengthen its position.

At present, most serious fourth generation efforts come from the periphery and conflict between these regions and the empire which is for the most part centered in the West has existed for centuries, of course. So there's nothing particularly new going on there. However, within the center of the empire there does seem to be a separation taking place due to a lack of cultural cohesion. In Europe, the conflict is fueled by mass immigration into what were until very recently mostly homogenous societies. In America, I think the conflict is largely a class conflict on two different levels. First, there is the broader widening of class divisions that has simultaneously generated a strengthened plutocracy at the top, a shrinking middle class and a growing lower proletarian and lumpenproletarian class. Large scale immigration has played a role in this obviously, but I don't think it's the principal cause. Second, there seems to be a particularly intense class struggle between the dying WASP elites and their constituents among the traditional middle class and the rising upper middle class that is informed by the values of political correctness or what I call totalitarian humanism. This is what I consider to be the source of the US culture wars.

S: I think what you call "totalitarian humanism," I call liberalism without the gloves on. This, however, confuses people since the term liberal is linked to the center-left, which is only one of its manifestations. Do you see the contradictions within totalitarian humanism leading to more or less balkanization?

K.P.: Oh, more balkanization, very much so. In fact, I think the contradictions within totalitarian humanism will be what will eventually cause its demise. Totalitarian humanism will end when the PC coalition fractures and its component parts eventually turn on each other. A key fault line is going to be the incompatibility of Western liberalism with the social conservatism endemic to most non-Western cultures. For instance, I've seen some research that shows anti-gay attitudes are more prevalent among African-Americans than any other ethnic group in the US. Secularism is certainly far more prevalent among Western liberals than among Third world immigrants. Right now, the line that the totalitarian humanist Left takes is something along the lines of "Oppressed peoples everywhere, unite against the white bourgeoisie!" or some variation of that. But these fault lines are very real and will increasingly find their way to the surface over time.

S.: Is this why you have done so much work with alt right? That the Marxist and anarchist left no longer distances itself from liberalism in a meaningful way?

K.P.: I'd say there are four things that drew me towards the alt right. First, the alt right is about 100% consistently opposed to American imperialist military adventurism. The Left often falls down on this question and gets taken in by supposed "humanitarian interventions," for instance. The alt right also has a strong Nietzschean foundation which overlaps quite well with my own philosophical and meta-political stance. The alt right is much more willing to critique or criticize Christianity in a way that would be unthinkable to American-style conservatives and in a way that offers a lot more depth than the reflexive secular humanism or theological liberalism found on the Left. Lastly, as you point out, the alt right is the only political tendency that consistently criticizes totalitarian humanism and does so in a penetrating way.

I consider totalitarian humanism to be a very dangerous force that is on the rise in the West, and despite their professed oppositional stance, the Marxist and anarchist left have swallowed the totalitarian humanist bait hook, line, and sinker so to speak, essentially making them the useful idiots of the liberal establishment.

S.: A friend of mine says the same thing: "Lately the rhetoric between liberals and leftist, you'd think the far left would be an alternative to a lot of PC platitudes, but it isn't anymore." This leads me to some serious questions: I have noticed a lot of professed anti-Fascists using fascist-style intimidation against other forms of anarchism. I suspect you see these anarchists essentially reflecting the anarcho-liberal confusion and becoming a sort of militant-wing for liberal identity politics?

K.P.: The "anti-fascists" are the mirror image of the Nazi storm troopers who went about physically attacking Jews and Marxists during the Weimar period. Essentially they are the brown shirts of totalitarian humanism. The tendencies that I refer to as the "anarcho-leftoids" are a kind of parody of PC. Describing them as a "militant wing for liberal identity politics" would be apt in some ways, though perhaps too charitable. They are the new fascists in every essential aspect.

Your question here brings up a very important point. I've stated before that my ultimate goal is to build a kind of confederation or agglomeration of tribes of anarchists, libertarians, and other anti-authoritarian radicals who may have many, many profound differences of opinion or ways of life but who are united in their commitment to attacking the state. And, of course, I've developed the concept of pan-secessionism as a tactic to be used towards that end. I am sometimes asked if whether my persistent criticisms of the left-anarchists in these areas are not antithetical to my larger goal of a unified anarchist resistance. Am I not acting as a divider rather than as a bridge-builder?

But the immediate problem that we are confronted with is the fact that this totalitarian leftist mindset dominates the mainstream of the anarchist movement, certainly in the English-speaking countries. The leftist-anarchists insist on excluding the other anarchist tribes from their midst on the ground that they are not pure enough in doctrine. For instance, anarcho-capitalists, national-anarchists, Tolkienesque anarcho-monarchists, Nietzschean anarchists of the right, religious anarchists, conservative anarchists similar to the late Joe Sobran, sometimes even left-libertarians like the agorists, mutualists, or voluntaryists are rejected for their supposed deviance from official doctrine in one way or another. The leftist fundamentalism that dominates the mainstream anarchist movement is comparable in many ways to the Protestant fundamentalism that dominates American Christianity. I know because I've been both a Protestant fundamentalist and a left-anarchist at various points in my life.

So I'm in a situation where in order to pursue my long-terms goals of unifying anti-state radicals against our common enemy, it's necessary to become a divider in the short-term. I'm divisive because I attack the grip that doctrinaire leftism has on the movement, particularly in the USA. Whenever you speak out against the prevailing trend, you automatically become a divisive figure. So of course those within the mainstream anarchist movement will often come to regard someone like me as the equivalent of heretic who has rejected articles of the true faith. But then there are other anarchists who start to think, "Well, you know, maybe Preston has a point with some of his criticisms" and maybe I provide a platform for those anarchists who are aware of some of these problems and have been hesitant to speak up. I'm also opening the door for those anarchists whose own beliefs differ from those of the hard leftists to eventually become accepted by and integrated into the wider anarchist milieu. There are a number of trends in left-anarchism that I see as encouraging such as the post-leftist, situationist, and Stirner-influenced tendencies. While I have my differences with primitivists I have not found them to be as hostile towards other types of anarchists as the leftoids. I also very much appreciate those anarchist tendencies that assert a kind of tribal identity among minority ethnic groups, such as Anarchist People of Color or native anarchists. This is of course very consistent with my broader goal of building a confederation of anti-state tribes.

S.: Do you see the tribe as the only viable and possibly just political unit?

K.P.: I should probably clarify what I mean by "tribe." I'm using the term as a metaphor for any kind of voluntary association sharing a common purpose or identity and functioning independently of the state. So in this context there could certainly be anarchist "tribes" in the common sense of a population group sharing a particular language, culture, religion, or ethnicity, but there could also be tribes committed to a specific political stance, or economic system, or lifestyle interest. For instance, some years ago I came across a group advocating a "stoner homeland" for potheads in northern California. Presumably, there could be stoner anarchist tribes and there could be straight edge anarchist tribes just like there can be tribes representing Christians or Muslims or other kinds of identities. Within the anarchist tradition, for instance, I would consider syndicalists to be a tribe, the individualist-anarchists to be a tribe, the Kropotkinites to be a tribe, the Catholic Workers to be a tribe, and so forth.

I think tribes are the most natural form of human social organization. Therefore, they are probably the most viable in terms of durability as well. As to whether they are the most just, I think that's a subjective question. I don't really believe in the concept of abstract justice found in much of traditional Western metaphysics of the kinds associated with, for instance, Plato or the Church fathers or the natural rights theorists of the Enlightenment. I'm very much a Nietzschean, possibly a Foucaultian, on this question.

The Tyranny of the Politically Correct

S.: What do you think is Nietzsche's relevance to anarchism?

K.P.: Of all the great thinkers of the modern era, Nietzsche was probably the most prescient and penetrating. He recognized that the core foundations of Western civilization, whether philosophical, cultural, moral, religious, had essentially been overthrown by the advancements in human knowledge that came out of the scientific revolution, the industrial revolution, and the Enlightenment. Not only had Christianity been discredited, but so had traditional Western metaphysics. What distinguishes the thought of Nietzsche is that he takes things a step further and attacks the intellectual systems that grew out of the Enlightenment and had taken hold among educated people in his own era. In particular, he understood the progressive faith associated with movements like liberalism and socialism to essentially be secular derivatives of Christianity. Nietzsche regarded the intellectuals of his time as not having really abandoned faith in God, but rather as having invented new gods to believe in like progress, utopianism, equality, universalism, nationalism, racialism, anarchism, and so forth. All of these became forms of secular millenarianism in Nietzsche's day.

Nietzsche considered all of these trends to be efforts to come to terms, or perhaps avoiding coming to terms, with the death of the foundations of traditional values. He saw these new gods as creating a cultural powder keg that would explode in grotesque warfare in the twentieth century, which is precisely what happened. He also believed it would be the twenty-first century before Western people began to really confront the crisis generated by the erosion of the foundations of their civilization and that cultural nihilism would be the greatest obstacle that the West would have to overcome. We see this today in the self-hatred and wish for cultural self-destruction that exists among Western peoples, particularly the educated elite. For instance, it is quite obviously seen in the thrill with which Western intellectuals anticipate the potential demographic overrun and cultural dispossession of the West.

What is ironic is that the leftist fundamentalism that dominates the mainstream of the anarchist milieu is perhaps the most advanced form of this nihilism. They've essentially absorbed the nihilism of the Western elites and amplified it several times over. In particular, they often epitomize the slave morality Nietzsche regarded as having its roots in Christianity and having been carried over into its secular derivatives on the political left.

So I think that the thought of Nietzsche, properly understood, could contribute to an awakening in the anarchist community, and provide us with the intellectual armor necessary to effectively combat our establish overlords rather than simply parroting them as so many of us do now. It does no good to simply regurgitate the values of political correctness when these are simultaneously the legitimizing values of the ruling class.

S.: Thank you for your time. Anything you'd like to say in closing?

K.P.: Just to say that the first principal of any authentic radicalism has to be independence of mind above all other values. It's not about how much you agree or disagree with me. Rather, it's about your ability to apply critical analysis to every question and to every situation. It's about being able to see every side of every question and giving due recognition where it's merited. Any set of ideas, no matter what they are, can become menacing when they are dogmatized to the point of becoming unquestionable articles of faith, particularly when intertwined with the authority of the state. No matter how righteous a particular crusade may seem if its presumptions are not subject to regular critical scrutiny then it becomes a potential foundation for yet another tyranny.

12

On Feminism

An interview with Keith Preston on Feminism, Anarchism, and National-Anarchism

What is your opinion on feminism and how it has impacted American women?

Any discussion of feminism has to begin with the recognition that feminism contains within itself many different strands, as is the case with any ideological tradition, whether anarchism, socialism, or nationalism. Like any other ideology, the focus, emphasis, or definition of "feminism" has varied widely at different times. For instance, feminism today is identified or associated with the radical Left, but a pioneer feminist, Josephine Butler, was part of what would today be called the religious right and a number of leaders of the suffragist movement in England later became supporters of Oswald Mosley's British fascist movement. Historians of feminism will generally divide Western feminism into three successive "waves": the early women's rights activists and the suffragettes of the late 19th/early 20th century, the "women's lib" movement that came out of 1960s radicalism, and a newer trend called "third wave" that's roughly twenty years old. As to what my opinion of feminism is, that would also vary widely depending on the time and topic being discussed. I generally have a positive view of the movement for women's rights that came out of British and by extension American classical liberalism in the 19th century. This was a movement to gain legal and economic rights for women like the right to own property or engage in contracts, and to have greater rights to their children. Previously, women had chattel status within the context of families and marriage and were often regarded legally and culturally as the property of their fathers or husbands. It's the same kind of arrangement that still more or less exists in other parts of the world today, with somewhere like Saudi Arabia or Afghanistan being an extreme example. I regard the relatively high status of women in Western cultures compared with other places to be one of the many great achievements of Western civilization.

As for the movement to grant voting rights to women, I have mixed feelings about it. I am skeptical of mass democracy in general, on anarchist as well as elitist grounds, and some of the early anarchist-feminists like Emma Goldman expressed reservations about suffrage, believing middle class liberal and socialist women would use the vote to expand the power of the state. For instance, the women's vote had much to do with the passage of Prohibition, which was a ridiculous and disastrous policy. Women's political groups have often been strong supporters of the nanny state, though I think that shows the limitations of the thinking of the times, whether past or present, and not any limitations that are inherent to women. I don't think suffrage per se was the problem, as much as the fact that it was granted during the time of the growth of mass democracy and the modern leviathan state that we are still struggling with. Even with these criticisms, however, I generally regard first wave feminism as a positive thing, and of course I would certainly favor equal political and legal rights for all women within the context of a decentralized, tribal, anarchic, libertarian or communitarian system.

"Second wave" feminism of the kind that came out of the 60s and 70s I have a much more critical view of. On one hand, it raised a lot of valid and reasonable issues, like pervasive discrimination against women in things like employment and education. It also addressed some serious social issues like violent crimes such as rape and domestic assault perpetrated against women. But the so-called "women's lib" movement of the time also adopted the Cultural Marxist outlook that regards sexual differentiation as oppression by definition, and considers men to be an oppressor class that hereby becomes defined as the enemy. The consequence of this is that the modern feminist movement has become a core component of the Cultural Marxist program to attack Western civilization as nothing more than a legacy of white male heterosexual oppression. Further, by defining men as an enemy class, feminists have sought to dramatically expand the power of the state ostensibly in the name of waging war against patriarchy in the economic and cultural sphere. Additionally, in those spheres where feminists have become institutionally powerful, a notorious example being the family court system, the Cultural Marxist framework has been used to implement abusively anti-male policies, including the virtual criminalization of fathers, comparable to the efforts by "anti-racists" to perpetrate racism against whites in other sectors.

Feminist tendencies associated with the "third wave" I have a cautiously sympathetic view of. Third wave emerged in part as a corrective to the excesses of the second wave, and it appears to be much less inclined towards misandry and less statist and authoritarian than its predecessor, but it's a young movement so it's difficult to guess where it will actually lead.

In terms of how feminism has impacted American women, on the positive side historic feminist movements have gained greater legal, political, and economic rights for women, and greater opportunities in the professions and education, and have raised serious issues that were sometimes ignored or overlooked in the past. The problem has not been feminism per se in every conceivable form, but the particular form that Western feminism has taken since at least the 1960s, perhaps earlier, where it has become aligned with Marxism, anti-Western and anti-European ethno-masochism, racism against whites, misandry, and its alliance with the state. Nowadays, we even see aggressive warfare being defended on feminist grounds like the case of Trotskyist-turned-neoconservative Christopher Hitchens' professed desire to bomb the Afghans out of the Stone Age. That's more or less the rationale the Soviets used for their own Afghan war.

Those are the political problems. In the cultural realm, the problem with the way feminism has evolved is that by seeking to eliminate sexual differentiation it has not only sought to defy basic biological science, but to devalue social and cultural roles traditionally occupied by women. For instance, one of the classic works of second wave feminism is Betty Friedan's *The Feminine Mystique* which argues that women who devote themselves to tasks like child-rearing are living unfulfilling lives. When I was growing up in the 70s and 80s I used to hear housewives and stay-at-home moms referred to as "non-persons" by feminists, as if childcare and home maintenance are somehow unimportant or insignificant activities. In academic feminist circles today, you will hear talk about supposed "gender segregation by occupation" in the economic world, meaning that men and women tend to be disproportionately concentrated in different kinds of professions and occupations. Implicit in this is the idea that women can find happiness only by becoming carbon copies of men. There's no room for feminine identity of any kind, not only in the biological sense of reproductive roles, but in the cultural and social realm as well. Feminists will complain that these kinds of differentiation exist not only in relatively traditional or conservative societies like Japan but even in uber-liberal ones like the Scandinavian countries. But what that indicates is that there are indeed innate differences between males and females that cannot be repealed by legal degree or ideological fantasy. I think a consequence of this is that while women may have advanced in certain areas, they've lost out in others. For instance, traditionally males were expected to be able to care for their wives and children, and the characteristics women looked for in males were things like personal responsibility, reliability, dependability, a work ethic, and so forth. Nowadays, it's more or less expected that women will have to make their own way when it comes to making a living and raising children. I think that's lowered the standards considerably concerning what women will accept in spouses, lovers, and relationship partners. For instance, I've always been amazed at the number of attractive, intelligent, seemingly competent, reasonably successful or self-sufficient women who hook up with guys who are total losers or scumbags, and I think the reason for this often amounts to a lack of expecting anything better.

How has it impacted the American populace overall? Do you have an opinion on how it has affected Western Civilization?

Some people have argued that feminism has contributed to the breakdown of the stability of the family and has contributed to resulting social pathologies in the process. I think there's some partial truth in that. When I was in elementary school in the early 70s, most families I knew were ones where the father made a living and the mother raised the children. Maybe the mom had a part time job as well. There was a minority of families where both parents were full time working people or were divorced or where the kids were being raised by a single parent, and the kids spent most of their time in daycare or being farmed out to relatives. The interesting thing is that it always seemed to be those kids who were screwed up, got in fights, stole, set fires, engaged in petty mischief, and all that. Nowadays, most kids grow up among divorces, single parenthood, or are raised in large part by babysitters and day care professionals. So I suspect it's true that less stable families have produced more pathological children. I don't think the blame for this can be laid solely at the feet of feminists, however. There have also been significant changes in the economy that require most households to have two incomes, for instance. The nature of the economy has also eradicated traditional communities, and people have become a lot less rooted. Nowadays, people change jobs or relocate every few years or even every few months. They don't even know who their neighbors are, and that doesn't contribute much stability to a child's life.

What changes would you like to see in regards to feminism's effect on American society?

I'd like to see an end to misandry on the part of feminists, and recognition of the legitimacy of differentiation among the sexes. Misandry is not the solution to misogyny anymore than ethno-masochism or anti-white racism is the solution to more traditional forms of racism. I'd like to see an end to feminism's alliance with the state and with Cultural Marxism.

What other options are available for American women who do not like their current situation?

That would depend on what their situation is. The starting point answer I would give is the same I would give to a male who does not like his current situation: "What can you do to help yourself? Whom else can you seek out who can help you when you can't help yourself?"

In what way can National-Anarchism provide solutions? How do tribes and autonomous communities benefit women?

In the broader ideological sense, National-Anarchism opposes both the state and Cultural Marxism, which puts it at odds with a great deal of feminism as feminism is presently constituted. I think that may well change over time. Some of the younger feminists associated with things like the third wave or post-feminism have rejected at least some of the excesses of their predecessors. Also, Cultural Marxism will lose a lot of its sympathizers the more it reveals its fangs and the more imminent dramatic demographic change in the West becomes. I think a lot of former liberals and leftists will eventually decide that Western civilization and white people aren't so bad after all given the alternatives, and I think many of them will find National-Anarchism as a preferable alternative to the reactionary, theocratic, or fascist variations of the Right.

At the broadest level, National-Anarchism benefits women because National-Anarchism seeks to preserve and maintain Western civilization where women have achieved higher status than anywhere else. On a more immediate level, the ideas of tribe and community serve as a corrective for the uprooting of traditional communities that has occurred at the hands of the state, capitalism, and other characteristics of modern life like technology and high mobility. The formation of National-Anarchist tribes serves as a means of at least partially restoring the traditional communities that have been lost, or at least providing a viable substitute. Also, I think that tribes and communities are potential sources of support for women on a wide range of matters that are currently provided for by the state or by capitalist institutions. Kevin Carson, Sean Gabb, Kirk Sale, myself and others who theorize about what sorts of economic arrangements might arise in the absence of the state or plutocratic institutions propped up by the state have suggested that workers bargaining power would increase dramatically and that the number and variety of economic enterprises would likewise experience profound expansion. This would provide more options for everyone, including women, as to how to go about making a living, and allow for more personal independence and self-sufficiency and more stable communities and families. Kevin Carson, for instance, has also written about the kinds of mutual aid societies that existed before the rise of the welfare state. These may be a proto-type for the provision of such services by communities and tribes following the future demise of the state.

What roles and functions do you see women playing within the National-Anarchist scene?

A revolutionary movement should be a proto-type for what a future society would look like. The characteristics of a revolutionary movement are an indication of what kind of future social system it will establish. I'm in favor of an aristocracy of merit where everyone rises according to their efforts and abilities, including women, of course. I'd be very much in favor of a National-Anarchist movement where women were heavily represented among its leadership and public figures.

Some years ago I used to do a live call-in talk show on public access television. Over time, I noticed that if I was discussing topics like government, law, economics, war, or foreign policy, then ninety percent of the callers would be male. But when the topics of discussion switched to health or health care, education, children, psychology, interpersonal relationships, religion, crime, the environment, matters of social or cultural relations like race, or comparable issues, the callers were divided about fifty percent between men and women, with women occasionally becoming dominant among the callers depending on the topic. The lesson I took from that experience is that women are geared, whether through socialization or innate qualities or both, to be able to better relate to certain parts of the human experience where men relate more easily to other parts. This would seem to be an important part of the differentiation that does indeed exist between the sexes.

I don't see women as playing either a subordinate role or as rivals to men in the National-Anarchist scene. Rather, I see males and females as partners in common projects and common objectives. That doesn't mean there can't be differences of focus at times. For instance, over a lengthy period of time I would like to see National-Anarchists and allied movements develop their own network of social institutions that would ultimately serve to replace the role of the welfare state in society at large. I would like to see our movements create our own schools, health clinics, child care systems, systems of relief for the poor, elderly, disabled, or homeless, efforts to assist battered women or abused children, victims of rape and other violent crimes, assistance to young girls who become pregnant, aid for runaway or throwaway kids, assistance to drug addicts and alcoholics, and other comparable activities. My guess based on past observation and experience is that women are naturally more drawn to helping professions and charitable activities than men, probably because their reproductive roles bring with them a greater genetic inclination to engage in nurturing activities. I don't view such activities as secondary to the "important stuff" like politics, business, and war, but as an essential foundation of any decent kind of society.

At the same time, I think the ability of women to contribute to traditionally "male-dominated" areas of human life is often grossly underestimated. For instance, in the mainstream of American society there is a debate about the role of women in the military. While I honor those who join the military with honest or honorable motivations, I don't really think anyone should join the military at present, because it serves to wage war on behalf of a corrupt, tyrannical, and destructive regime. That said, having done a great deal of research on armed insurgent movements in places like Asia, Latin America, or the Middle East, I think there's little doubt that women can often perform so-called "man's work" like soldiering with a great deal of skill and talent.

What functions do female members fulfill in your organization/ tribe?

What I try to do is gather around myself a collection of superior individuals who can become the foundation of a future revolutionary movement inspired by the ideas of National-Anarchism and overlapping or allied tendencies or movements. I don't approach this is a gender-specific way. I favor an aristocracy based on individual merit that is gender-neutral. The people who have come into my circle have been overwhelmingly male thus far. I think a lot of that has to do with the particular stage of development our groups and movements are at right now. I think more women will become involved over time as we are able to expand our range of activities and the issues we address. But the women in my political orbit tend to be extraordinarily impressive individuals, and I think we will likewise attract many more such women over time.

13

Reply to a Left-Anarchist Critic

A left-anarchist posted this critique of American Revolutionary Vanguard/Attack The System on another forum. I've included the critic's comments in italics followed by my own comments in response.

Really analyze the mission statement in its totality. First and foremost it constructs the Anarchist movement in a particular manner, like the most vulgar An-Caps and Libertarians, Preston cites "anti-statism" as the defining aspect of Anarchism.

From Webster's Ninth New Collegiate Dictionary: Anarchism /'an-er-,kiz-em/ noun (1642) 1. a political theory holding all forms of governmental authority to be unnecessary and undesirable and advocating a society based on voluntary cooperation and free association of individuals and groups. 2. the advocacy or practice of anarchism.

But this is no surprise given that Preston was a contributor to anti-state.com, the Anarcho-Capitalist website, so it's not difficult to understand where he draws his reasoning on this one. His assertion is incorrect, as has been said more than once here, Anarchism has never been reducible to "anti-statism" and is much broader, having declared its opposition to all forms of rulership. This is what, apparently, allows Preston to adopt the label with such zeal. If anyone objects, he and his supporters can start the "I'm more hardcore than you" debate about his interpretation being more "pure" than yours.

From the Oxford Dictionary: ruler 1. a person or agent exercising government or control. The critic offers no explanation of how "rulership" is to be differentiated from "the state" or "government."

In almost the same breath, Preston attempts to distinguish himself from both the Left and the Right, by rejecting the labels of "Third Positionism and White Nationalism" while rejecting the Left and its goals of a fair society for all, in its entirety.

109

Reply to a Left-Anarchist Critic

I do indeed distinguish myself from both Left and Right in that I oppose the reactionary, conservative, or bourgeoisie manifestations of the Right, while borrowing selectively from strands of "rightist" thought such as those I recognized in my exchange with Paul Gottfried: natural inequality of persons at both the individual and collective levels, the inevitability and legitimacy of otherness, the superiority of organic forms of human organization over social engineering, rejection of vulgar economism, and a tragic view of life. As for the Left, I consider the classical liberal and classical anarchist strands of the Left to be among the primary influences on my own thinking, while rejecting the Jacobin, Marxist, or Marcusean manifestations of the Left. While recognizing what I consider to be the legitimate issues raised by white nationalists and attempting to incorporate these into my own paradigm, I reject white nationalism as an ideological system, as it is essentially a form of egalitarian collectivism ("racial Marxism"). But then I do the same with black nationalism, American Indian nationalism, Puerto Rican nationalism, Palestinian nationalism, Tibetan nationalism, etc. Third Positionism is a term for ideologies that reject both capitalism and communism and which advocate a "third position" between these two. These include many different ideologies from all over the world. It has its roots in systems of thought like old British distributism and today it's an umbrella term that includes all sorts of unrelated philosophies, ranging from Peronism to Ba'athism to the ideas in Qadaffi's "Green Book" to the political and economic aspects of Ghandi's *satyagraha* philosophy to strands of Islamic economic thought. Some neo-fascists in Europe have also latched onto the term which is the obvious source of the leftist hysteria over it. Here's a good way to look at it: Libertarianism is neither left nor right in that it opposes both conservative as well as leftist forms of statism. There are also anti-capitalist and pro-capitalist forms of libertarianism. Likewise, Third Positionism is neither left or right in that it opposes both capitalism and communism, and there are statist and anti-statist variations of third positionism. So a technically proficient application of political language would indicate that I am both a libertarian and a third positionist, given my radical anti-statism and my free-market syndicalist-mutualist-distributist-communitarian economic outlook.

The idea that the Left is merely about a "fair society for all" is lunacy. This ignores the authoritarian and totalitarian strands of the Left. It ignores the bloody history of the Left in some countries. There's also the question of how "fair" is to be defined in the first place. Nor do I reject all goals normally associated with the Left. A comprehensive

110

review of Attack the System and my various published writings will reveal that I have incorporated the great majority of the conventional left-anarchist program into my own paradigm, including a lot of issues that are shockingly radical even by conventional leftist or liberal standards (e.g. prison abolition, abolition of compulsory education, drug user and sex worker rights). My critics who have anything beyond a peripheral familiarity with my work are no doubt well aware of this. Their attacks on me are nothing more that willful and knowing lies and slander, because they don't want my arguments to be heard.

A first principle of anarchism is that we should be freethinkers above all. This means that we do not simply approach issues on the basis of what the party line of the Left is at present, or what our PC professors told us, or what we pulled off of Infoshop.Org. Instead, it means that all issues and matters of controversy must be evaluated on their own terms, with an attitude of civility towards all but those devoid of incivility, and a fair hearing for all contending points of view, on which no one is to have the last word. Further, it means that issues have to be examined within the context of their relationship to anarchism, not leftism. For instance, when members of the racial minority, feminist, and "LGBT" communities or other conventional constituencies for the Left raise claims of oppression, by all means we should give their arguments a fair hearing. But we should do the same for all other demographic and political interest groups. We then need to evaluate whether claims of oppression are legitimate within the context of the anarchist political and philosophical paradigm. Much of the time they are. Sometimes they are not. For instance, sexual minorities who claim they are oppressed by sodomy laws, legal repression of gay-oriented businesses, or violent crimes by private individuals who target them on the basis of their gender or sexual identity are legitimate within the anarchist paradigm. Neo-Nazis who claim they are oppressed by the mere existence of Jews are not legitimate. Racial separatist whites (or of any other race/ethnicity) who claim their rights of property and association are being violated by discrimination prohibition are legitimate. Feminists who would legally require churches to accept women into the ranks of the clergy are not as this violates the associational and religious liberties of others. At the same time, there would be nothing inherently un-libertarian about feminists within a church organization agitating for altering church policy regarding gender exclusivity in the clergy if they so desired.

There are a lot of issues where there is much gray area. These include the familiar issues where there is no clear agreement among anarchists and libertarians such as abortion, capital punishment, animal rights, children's rights against their parents, the limits of self-defense, the handling of predatory criminals, the precise definitions of property rights, the use of the environment, and so forth. There are other issues as well. For instance, if private discrimination against particular demographic groups (races, religions, cultures, genders, sexual orientations, occupations), even if not legally required, is so pervasive as to severely undermine the economic, social, or even physical health of those on the receiving end of such discrimination, then what sorts of remedies may be in order? These may be situations where the Ghandi-MLK paradigm becomes applicable, e.g. people using their liberties of speech, assembly, association, trade, boycott, etc. as a means of opposing or at least reducing such discrimination. There is also the issue of how to apply anarchist theory in societies like our own where the state and state-protected institutions dominate much of the society. With regards to discrimination, for instance, it would seem reasonable enough that government, service providers with a state-protected monopoly, or mass corporations created by the state should not be able to deny services or protection to individuals and groups for arbitrary or irrelevant reasons. For instance, the US Postal Service should not be able to provide mail delivery only for whites but not for blacks, and public schools should not be able to provide admission only to Protestants but not to Catholics. Nor should General Motors be able to refuse to hire Mormons or gays simply because they are Mormons or gays.

There may be some instances where there are simply irreconcilable differences between those making claims of oppression and where both sides present valid and compelling arguments. One of these is the traditional tension between left and right wing anarchists over the "right to work" versus the "right to strike." To what degree are employers legitimate in replacing striking workers with "scabs"? To what degree are workers legitimate in preventing scabbing? Right-anarchists are typically "pro-scab" while left-anarchists are usually "anti-scab." The former will argue in favor of freedom of contract, freedom of movement, property rights, freedom of association, etc. The latter will argue against the employer's claims that its position is legitimate and that workers are the rightful owners of their jobs. I find both sides of this issue compelling and my guess is that a libertarian legal code would largely reflect prevailing regional and local ideological currents on this question, e.g. the degree to which scabbing is legally tolerated or the degree to which scabbing is prohibited, and the degree to which extra-legal means of preventing scabbing are tolerated (e.g. civil disobedience). Immigration is another such issue.

The Tyranny of the Politically Correct

I've made my criticisms of some of the "open borders" libertarians and anarchists known in the past, but not all issues raised by proponents of "immigrants' rights" are foolish or illegitimate, either. Again, this is why I've suggested that in an anarchist polity with a libertarian legal code matters of immigration and naturalization would likely be a local matter with varying degrees of restrictiveness or permissiveness on this question. I myself would likely prefer some degree of moderation on this question.

He simplifies the politics of the "New Left" and "Old Left" and places them into a dichotomy.

This is a standard practice of historians of the Left from all sorts of ideological perspectives. It did not originate with me.

Anyone who responds to or criticizes ATS or Preston can then be labeled a "Leftist" or "Leftoid" which dismisses the criticism without actually having to make a meaningful response.

The term "leftoid" was one I coined about twenty years ago as a derivative of "Stalinoid." I have always used it to describe the reflexive dogmatism and cultic psychology common to so much of the Left. I have indeed made many a "meaningful response" to my critics. They're just not listening. Instead, they hear what they want to hear.

It's a duck and weave and all those who openly espouse discriminatory attitudes and behaviors can cheer from the sidelines.

The critic gives no explanation of what he means by "discriminatory attitudes." I presume he's not describing left-liberals who wish to discriminate against gun owners or Communists who wish to discriminate against small property owners or militant secularist or gay rights activists who wish to discriminate against religious believers or "anti-racists" who wish to discriminate against ethnic Europeans, or academic leftists who discriminate against conservative student groups who wish to form organizations on college campuses. Clearly, none of these classes of discriminating individuals are fans of my work. Therefore, it is unclear why this critic would say that "all those who openly espouse discriminatory attitudes and behaviors" are cheering me on from the sidelines.

More to the point, Preston claims that populism determines class identities.

113

No. What I argue is that Anarchism tends to identify class struggle in terms of "the people versus the elite" while the Marxists see class struggle in the more reductionist manner of wage laborers versus employers, property owners, or holders of capital. This insight is not original to me. I picked it up from Larry Gambone, whose left-anarchist credentials are impeccable. The populist struggle against the elite transcends class identities in that it does not rely on a single class as a principal agent (like the Marxists do with their deification of the proletariat). That said, I have indeed identified particular class identities that I describe as the "vanguard classes" in an anarchist struggle in a contemporary society.

> *according to Preston and every Third Positionist out there, "the Left are in power", therefore the Right are anti-establishment and a more legitimate fighting force for "freedom".*

The present day ruling class paradigm is a synthesis of classical bourgeoisie liberalism and socialism (i.e. a capitalist/social democratic hybrid) and the institutionalization of the values of the cultural revolution of the 1960s and 1970s. Therefore, the Left is indeed "in power." The Right is anti-establishment in the sense of opposing the dominant liberal-left paradigm. As to whether the Right is "a more legitimate fighting force for freedom," that depends on which strands of the Right we are talking about. Some strands of the Right are flagrantly anti-freedom. Some are stridently pro-freedom (e.g. the Rothbardians). Most are a mish-mash of pro-freedom and authoritarian ideas (just like the different strands of the Left).

> *In doing this Preston represents his views, and by extension, the views of others on the Right as being consistent with the views of the people, or alternatively, being on the side of "ordinary people", which works as an attempt to justify or legitimate his ideas. Apparently, anyone who declares "Fight da powa!" is a class warrior, a representative of the people, and their ideas are justifiable no matter the content or ramifications.*

No. The "views of the people" are probably closer to the center than anywhere else (that's why it's called the center). Most research shows that "ordinary people" are to the right of the elites on cultural and social issues, but to the left of the elites on economic issues, and more inclined towards foreign policy non-interventionism that the elites. There's no inherent relationship between populism and Fascism or Nazism, as the critic tries to suggest with his link. Populism can

114

be used towards any end, from fascism to communism to religious fundamentalism to nationalism to anarchism.

He then goes on to develop the idea of "anti-statism" saying, as a strategic goal that the existence of the State is the first and foremost priority.

An anarchist suggests that opposition to the state should be first priority of anarchism? Geez, who would have ever thought?!!

He rejects all other forms of oppression. As has been said by others, according to Preston, all other forms of oppression can wait until after the revolution. However this shows a shallow understanding of and Anarchism; if you are Anarchist and you oppose all forms of rulership, you oppose all forms of rulership, everywhere, consistently. Oppression is interconnected and can all be related back to authoritarianism. You have to keep the bigger picture in mind.

No. An honest reading of the full volume of my work would indicate that I have incorporated a wide assortment of issues of resistance to oppression into my broader ideological and strategic framework. These include the struggle for self-determination for indigenous ethnic minorities in the US (e.g. African-Americans, Natives/American Indians), opposition to American aggression against other peoples all over the world, opposition to oppression inflicted on a broad array of marginalized populations that even conventional leftists typically ignore, and struggle by and on behalf of the lowest socio-economic elements in the class system. There is the wider question of how to approach these questions in a way that is strategically feasible.

....'revolution is not driven by White Hetero Men who sit around drawing up plans about how to throw off the state (smoking, probably) while the women are out the back making the coffee, LGBT people are beaten in the street out the front, the KKK is erecting crosses in your neighbours front yard and those living across the street are arming themselves to the teeth in order to kill those "Islamo-fascist-Muslim-terrorists".'

This is so silly that it merits the dignity of a response only because these comments are fairly representative of the outlook of the leftoid cult. Someone who thinks that this is representative of American society, let alone general Western civilization, at the present juncture is simply a deluded nutcase who's stuck in a time warp where it's always 1968. Get with the times, dude! In a libertarian legal order, burning crosses on the front yards of other people without their consent would constitute the crimes of trespassing, vandalism, intimidation, probably arson, and a good number of other things. Violent physical attacks on "LGBT" people would constitute the crimes of murder, assault, robbery, and the like. Preferably, neighbors would be "arming themselves to the teeth" for the purpose of resisting ordinary criminals, government functionaries and, if necessary, external invaders. And suffice to say that the circles of alternative anarchism are comprised of much more than "white hetero men" (with even some of us evil white hetero guys, like myself, being non-smokers!) and that the women in our circles contribute much more than simply "making coffee" (I hate coffee!).

The Poet and radical LGBT activist Staceyann Chin said during an interview,

> *...sometimes what we intend to do is to walk in and flip the script, so that we become the more powerful people and the other people become the less powerful. It's hard because sometimes I want black people to be in charge and some white people to be slaves. Sometimes I feel that way because shit is fucked up. But that's reactive politics. That's revenge, not social justice work. The hardest thing is the question of saving everybody at the same time. Because you see how many people that are oppressed and you see the interconnectivity of racism and sexism and you're like, "shit! I just wanna help these motherfuckers here who are under stress. Can't I just focus on these people, and just be a feminist and not an antiracist? Can we not talk about poverty now, because these people are being raped over here?" But the most successful revolutions that have happened throughout history are those revolutions that had groups working together, and where the people who were working against slavery were also feminists. Seeing the whole picture. I think that's what I do, what I attempt to do.*

Well, I actually agree with this. When have I ever endorsed rape? When I have ever endorsed poverty? When have I ever endorsed slavery?

> *And at first, this might all appear to be what Preston and Jeremy have both been saying, but you would be wrong as Preston and his broad coalition of "left and right" that "transcends ideology" explicitly states that they are not fighting for equality between individuals and actively rejects those who do as "oppressors of the Right".*

The critic gives no definition of what he means by "equality of individuals." If he means equality of legal and political rights in the classical liberal sense, then I would be for "equality of individuals." If he means the equality of individuals to rise or fall according to their own merit, without being hampered by statist, feudal, theocratic or capitalist institutions, then I would be for equality of individuals. If he means opposition to genuine systems of class or caste exploitation, then I am for equality of individuals. But if he means "equality" in the sense of equating the foolish with the wise, the ignorant with the educated, the stupid with the intelligent, the diseased with the healthy, the drunk and addicted with the sober, the amateurish with the professional, the neophytes with the experienced, the ugly with the beautiful, the incompetent with the capable, the undeserving with the meritorious, and the insane with the mentally healthy, then I am by no means for equality of individuals. As for the matter of "oppressors of the Right," I most certainly am in favor of the equality of all individuals to own firearms, smoke in pubs, practice religion, own property, join exotic cults, patronize a prostitute, take drugs, open a home school, skip school, drink beer at age nineteen, eat junk food, practice alternative medicine, eat meat, or read a "non de-niggerized" edition of Huckleberry Finn.

According to Preston and the wider NA viewpoint, identities are a virus that need to be segregated in order to ensure social cohesion.

I'm only a fellow traveler to NA. I'm actually a classical anarchist and my own "anarcho-pluralist" outlook is simply a modern version of "anarchism without adjectives." However, NAs if anything celebrate identities rather than regarding them as "viruses." NA is the polar opposite of old-fashioned segregation like Jim Crow, apartheid, Nuremberg Laws, etc. Rather, it champions self-determination for all ethno-tribal and ethno-cultural groups on the basis of free association.

Even name-dropping Kropotkin as evidence that it is possible for Anarchists to "agree with some things the Right has to say" is misleading...

Kropotkin's strategic outlook regarding anarchist organizing among common people was the same as mine. For instance, he opposed trying to teach peasants about things like atheism, rationalism, Darwinism, etc, and instead favored respecting their cultural and religious traditions while offering assistance on their own issues of concern like economic oppression and exploitation by the state and feudal landlords. And, if this means anything, Kropotkin's daughter Alexandra actually immigrated to the USA and became a Goldwater supporter while continuing to claim her family's anarchist heritage.

> ... as Kropotkin and Bakunin both rejected their aristocratic positions in favor of egalitarianism and Anarchism. They didn't take up the fight for Anarchism to defend their titles or privilege, just as no Anarchist with integrity will take up the pen or take to the street to fight for or protect their own privilege, or the privilege of a select group of people.

Fortunately, we don't have titled aristocrats in modern Western societies, or where we still do, they are toothless. What "privilege" is it that we alternative anarchists are defending? The critic gives no examples or illustrations. Are we defending the military-industrial complex? Seeking to uphold the American empire? Are we Ayn Randian-fans of the corporate overlords? Are we apologists for the bureaucratic overlords of the New Class? Do we heap praise on the elites of the media and the world of academia? Do we going around displaying slogans like "Support the Troops" or "Support Your Local Police"? Not that I can tell.

> This means no alliance is possible with the reactive Right which states, explicitly, as an aim and goal, to prevent people from safely being able to be themselves,

• You mean people who want to be "born-again" Christians, or join the Branch Davidians, or display a Confederate flag, or own a handgun, or smoke tobacco, or attend a pre-Vatican II mass, or express politically incorrect opinions, or attend a home school, or watch or participate in beauty pageants? There is no evidence we alternative anarchists or those among our allies who are from the Right wish to prevent anyone from doing any of this.

> or, who want to fight to keep their privileged existence.

No explanation has been offered as to how any of us are "privileged." Most of us are certainly privileged compared to our counterparts in many other parts of the world. Fortunately, most of us are also stridently opposed to the oppression inflicted on people of other nations and civilizations by our own ruling classes such as people in Iraq, Afghanistan, Palestine, Columbia, Latin America, Iran, northern Africa, Southeast Asia, etc. Fortunately, the lumpenproletarian orientation of ARV/ATS incorporates the interests of the most oppressed in our own societies into a wider ideological and strategic paradigm.

> *Understand that agreement on one or two points does not mean two parties agree politically, that is, agree on what ought to occur. Milk is white and so is chalk dust. Would you drink a glass of chalk dust?*

Not being Marxists or Jacobin fundamentalists, we recognize that different subsets of human beings will always have conflicting ideals as to what constitutes "the good." As anarchists and radical decentralists, most of us generally concur that such differences should be dealt with according to the principles of individual liberty, free association, pluralism and peaceful co-existence where possible, and decentralism, localism, secession, and mutual self-separation where not possible.

> *What is being done is a total re-writing of basic terms and phrases. This is called spin and propaganda and is made much easier in an American cultural environment where people are not well-educated in politics and terms and phrases have been spun so often and so frequently, by so many different parties, they almost have no meaning.*

This is a rather extraordinary statement coming from someone who displays the level of abuse of political terminology and ignorance of political history of this critic.

> *There is no synthesis of ideas in Preston's work, but a loose set of ideas cherry picked from Anarchism and incorporated into those of reactive politics, the politics and cultural attitudes of the Right.*

This is a highly selective and willfully ignorant reading and evaluation of my work.

> *Any claim to have transcended ideology is rendered moot, as the bulk of his argument is taken from the Right in reaction to the Left. The phrasing, the rhetoric, the language and the politics is designed to attract those of the Left, as well as Preston's personalized anecdotes about his former life as an Anarchist.*

As the statement of purpose says, ARV/ATS is a dissident tendency within North American anarchism specifically and Western anarchism generally that seeks to compensate for the conventional anarchist movement's failure to both develop an ideological and strategic paradigm that is actually relevant to a twenty-first century Western society, and to recognize the dangers posed by authoritarian leftism (in spite of the history of bloody conflict between anarchists and left-statists). This is simply a replay of the battle between Bakunin and Marx, between the Kronstadt rebels and the Bolsheviks, or between the Spanish anarchists and the Stalinists.

14

Reply to a Cultural Marxist Critic

A Leftist who uses the name of "Equus" posted a limited critique of Attack the System on Royce Christian's blog. This is my response.

Equus begins his rebuttal by offering a concise and helpful summary of the points of his refutation. I repeat it in full:

My objection to Third Positionism is that it first and foremost has an ahistorical approach inasmuch as it is leftist and only retroactively places itself there, using ideas and attitudes not formulated at the time of the conception of the left/right political spectrum. It claims to be neither left nor right and claims to be a synthesis of right and left ideas while rejecting the sole premise of left-wing ideology. Furthermore, it understands being anti-state as an ideological characteristic instead of a tactical characteristic; it would claim Anarchists and anti-government fascists are ideologically similar instead of correctly placing Anarchism as an ideology that opposes the state in the context of leftist politics. While it co-opts much of Anarchist rhetoric, it dismisses two key concepts: solidarity and community. Finally, it may not be an exclusively right-wing idea, but it provides an arena for people who oppose what Anarchists stand for to enter the conversation as legitimate actors and gives nothing back. I know little of Preston's personal political background, and it is both irrelevant and hard to make the case that he is knowingly undermining Anarchism with his support of the Third Position. Regardless, his ideas have only provided a dangerous utility to the right that must be understood.

Equus proceeds with a discussion of the origins of the left/right dichotomy:

First, we need to look at the origin of the left/right political spectrum to broaden our view. This first began in the French Parliament around the time of the revolution. Those who favored the monarchy sat in the right wing and those who opposed it sat in the left wing. The most radical opponents of Monarchism sat in a part of the left wing

121

referred to as "the mountain." Among them was PJ Proudhon, the first philosopher to describe himself as an Anarchist and to articulate what was most likely a widely held view (I phrase it this way because any adherence to a figure as the sole example of a philosophy is a failure of understanding, i.e. Proudhon was a sexist, but that does not mean sexism is inherent to Anarchism). So there we have the basic framework for what it means to be leftist or rightist in a historical context.

While I agree that this is an accurate description of the origins of the left/right model of the political spectrum, I would also insist that the facts associated with the origins of this model are by themselves an indication of both the archaic (and indeed reactionary) nature of that model and the problematic nature of its continued use. If Proudhon is to be our starting point in a discussion of the historical contexts of the evolution of anarchist thought (and I agree he would seem to be as good a starting point as any), then perhaps we should begin by attempting an honest understanding of his actual views. No competent historian denies that modern anarchism has its roots in the left-wing of the Enlightenment and in the radical socialist labor movement. But this does not mean that anarchism is not to be distinguished from numerous other, more dominant strands of thought that emerged within the intellectual milieus and during the time periods in question. Erik von Kuehnelt-Leddihn aptly summarized Proudhon's contributions to political thought:

> *His socialism was distributist rather than collectivist; the key word to his economic thinking is "mutualism." He was strongly opposed to economic liberalism because he feared bigness - the concentration of wealth, mammoth enterprises - yet he was equally an enemy of the omnipotent centralized state, which is at the root of most leftist thinking. Proudhon's numerous books are full of notions and ideas that any true lover of liberty or any true conservative could underwrite...He always remained a healthy anti-statist and a convinced anti-democrat...Proudhon and Marx both dreamed of a "withering away of the state." Marx sought to fulfill his ideas by revolutionary means, by the use of brute force, by the "dictatorship of the proletariat." Proudhon, on the other hand, was an "evolutionist": the right order of things should be discovered, not arbitrarily blueprinted. Socialism should come gradually...it should encompass the globe through the voluntary consent of the people...not under one centralized superstate, but in a federal system-by federations deeply rooted in local customs, institutions, and traditions..*

In other words, while Anarchism is clearly a product of Enlightenment thinking, it (or at least Proudhon's version of it) is a product of that strand of Enlightenment thinking that adheres to a constrained rather than unconstrained vision of humanity and the nature of human societies. These contending strands in modernist thought have been identified very well by Dr. Thomas Sowell, and cut across conventional ideological boundaries. Equus describes the historical development of the Left in these terms:

> *The Monarchy opposed by the left has gone on to be Capitalism (in the case of socialists), racism (in the case of the black power movement among others), sexism (in the case of feminists), and so on. A colloquial way of phrasing it would be that the left is "anti-establishment."*

I have no disagreement with this statement. Yesterday's liberalism is today's conservatism. Today's radicalism is tomorrow's establishment. But if the Left is to be defined as the "anti-establishment," then who in present day Western societies would constitute the "anti-establishment"? Capitalism began the process of overthrowing the old order centuries ago and is now well-established and has been for a very long time. Likewise, the classical socialist movement has become integrated into the establishment. Labor unions were once illegal in some countries, as were the socialist parties. Today, they are mainstream, respectable establishment institutions led by persons drawn from the middle to upper classes. Contemporary Western economies are a capitalist/socialist hybrid and bear no resemblance to the form of capitalism written about by the likes of Charles Dickens or Karl Marx. In more recent times, racism and sexism have likewise become established as the ultimate social and personal sins. The open promotion of racism is a criminal offense in many Western countries. Indeed, even perceptions of racism of an entirely dubious nature can lead to a confrontation with the law. Few things are more menacing to the careers of public figures than accusations of racism. Overtly supremacist ideologies such as Nazism or the beliefs of the members of the Ku Klux Klan have come to be regarded as the ultimate in evil. During the apartheid era, South Africa came to be regarded as the ultimate pariah state. Those perceived to have waged successful battles against racism, such as Martin Luther King, Ghandhi, or Nelson Mandela have come to be regarded as the greatest of saints. Whatever else one thinks of racists, clearly they are not establishment figures. Sexism remains somewhat less of a taboo than racism, but it is a taboo nevertheless. Even so prominent an establishment figure

123

as the president of the most elite of universities is not insulated from sanctions generated by accusations of sexism. In other words, proponents of capitalism, socialism, anti-racism, or anti-sexism have been absorbed into the political and cultural mainstream of Western societies. Far from being "anti-establishment," the *Left is now the establishment.*

Next we need to understand the basics of the sociological study of social inequality. Sociologists generally use two umbrella terms about social inequality: the conservative thesis and radical antithesis, which divides thinkers into two groups: structural functionalists or conflict theorists. Structural functionalists generally claim that stratification is functional, perhaps inevitable, or even natural and good. Conflict theorists generally state that inequality is to some extent a social construct and must be destroyed or at least minimized.

As one who is familiar with the variations of sociological theory, I would say this formulation by Equus contains two principal errors. The first implicitly postulates that structural functionalism and conflict theory are mutually exclusive. They are not. One could recognize that stratification does indeed serve a functional purpose, while simultaneously recognizing the conflicting nature between demographic, political, or socioeconomic groups within a society. Because stratification may include a functional dimension, this does not mean that conflict is absent. Indeed, recognition of this principle brings us to the second fundamental error in the above statement by Equus. He ignores a primary aspect of conflict theory. To quote one of my old textbooks on sociological theory from graduate school:

Any significant change in the distribution of resources that favors a subordinated group will lead to political conflict or violence aimed at redistributing advantages. In such conflicts, subordinate groups exploit the counter-ideologies they have employed to salvage their self-esteem, using them to delegitimize dominant ideologies. *When a previously disadvantaged group rises to power, it exploits its new position just as did the group or groups it has displaced.*

This is precisely the process we have seen unfolding in the Western countries over the past two centuries. Capitalism succeeds in throwing off the *ancien regime* and "exploited its new position" by creating modern systems of capitalist or state-corporate plutocracy. Anarchists are of course aware of this. Socialism was incorporated into the managerial states that emerged in the early to mid twentieth century, and "exploited its position" through the development of the "new class" bureaucracies that have come to dominate modern states. See Alvin Gouldner on this New Class and James Burnham on its origins. More recently, "anti-racists" (a term that should by no means be regarded as a synonym for actual racial minorities) have achieved so much phenomenal success that their ideology has become one of the primary articles of faith of the legitimating ideologies of post-Christian Western states. The "Anti-racists" are now "exploiting their position" in a wide assortment of ways. Hence, the prevailing political correctness we see in all institutions at present, and the emergence of previously unknown "criminal" offenses such as those prohibiting free speech ("hate speech"), free thought ("hate crimes"), or freedom of association (discrimination prohibition), and new systems of privilege for the politically connected (so-called "affirmative action," for instance). In a similar fashion, feminists are also a newly minted establishment force that is "exploiting its position." In the USA, for example, feminist domination of family courts has resulted in misandrist policies aimed at the criminalization of fathers merely for their male status. In those countries where feminists have achieved the greatest amount of power, such as Sweden and Iceland, they are "exploiting their position" for the purpose of persecuting men and subordinated classes of women alike. Most contemporary left-anarchists understand of course that capitalism has long been a status quo, establishmentarian institution. What they have failed to do is recognize that socialism, "anti-racism," and "anti-sexism" have subsequently become establishmentarian forces as well. That they continue to beat the drums so loudly for social movements that have long been incorporated into the state is indication of their current reactionary nature. Hence, contemporary left-wing anarchism is a reactionary force that acts as an appendage to the left-wing of the establishment.

Now we come to a statement by Preston:

(Regarding the assertion that Anarchism is opposed to all forms of authority) I regard this as a revisionist definition of anarchism and one that is difficult to glean from the writings of the founding fathers of anarchism given a proper understanding of their ideas in relation to the context of their times.

It is perhaps ironic that Preston claims this to be the revisionist definition. Anarchists have been in no position to revise this definition. The works of Anarchist authors are readily available on the internet or in a library for any interested party and Anarchists have been in no position to alter them or destroy them. Is it happenstance that throughout history we see Anarchists aligning themselves with other anti-authoritarian movements? Every, and I say this with the utmost conviction, every Anarchist revolution, action, or moment of success has been intertwined with an opposition to all hierarchy (it should be noted that it escapes the scope of this article to explain in depth what "anti-authority" has meant to Anarchists. Obviously a shoemaker is the authority on making shoes. Anarchists have not and do not oppose that notion of the word).

Equus' comment regarding the shoemaker indicates that even he recognizes a distinction between natural and legitimate forms of authority, and coercive and artificial ones. Certainly, anarchists have traditionally opposed "hierarchy" in the forms of hierarchical privilege traceable to the impositions of the state. It is more questionable as to whether anarchism is simply a synonym for egalitarianism taken to the level of outright social nihilism. Some observations of Proudhon should help to clarify this distinction:

The February Revolution replaced the system of voting by "classes": democratic Puritanism still was not satisfied. Some wanted the vote given to children and women. Others protested against the exclusion of financial defaulters, released jailbirds, and prisoners. One wonders that they did not demand the inclusion of horses and donkeys.

Democracy is the idea of the state without limits.

Money, money, always money - this is the crux of democracy.

Democracy is more expensive than monarchy; it is incompatible with liberty.

Democracy is nothing but the tyranny of majorities, the most execrable tyranny of all because it rests neither on the authority of a religion, nor on the nobility of a race, nor on the prerogatives of talent or property. Its foundation is numbers and its mask is in the name of the people.

Democracy is an aristocracy of mediocrities.

It would seem safe enough to conclude that the founding father of modern anarchism was indeed rather suspicious of the wild egalitarianism our friend Equus seems to be insisting on.

The Spanish Revolution of 1936 saw Social and Political revolution intertwined, with the Anarchists firmly declaring that neither supersedes the other.

Yes, of course, but a social revolution against what? It was a social revolution against those institutions of oppression and exploitation allied with the state, e.g. feudal land barons, capitalist plutocrats, the theocratic church, the military, the police, etc.

The Paris commune and French revolution saw Anarchists with convictions outside of opposition to the state.

When have I ever argued that Anarchists should not have convictions outside of opposition to the state? I, for example, am an atheist and have very strong anti-Christian views. Yet I do not feel the need to bring my atheist convictions into all of my political projects for a variety of reasons. In the modern countries we have separation of church and state. Elites do not take religion seriously. Intellectual culture is overwhelmingly secular. Popular religion is very ecumenical in nature. Even conservative or fundamentalist religion is quite liberal by historical standards or even contemporary world standards. The influence of organized religion continues to decline. The common people are the most religious, and are alienated by overt attacks on their sacred beliefs. This is hardly conducive to organizing them politically and economically. Overt hostility to religion tends to produce a conservative religious backlash. Hence, I do not incorporate the militant atheism of many of the classical anarchists into my own paradigm (even if I might agree with it personally) because I do not feel it is necessary and I regard such as strategically destructive in a modern society. There are plenty of other issues that I do fit into my paradigm that do indeed involve matters other than opposing the state. As I said in an earlier critique of the cultural Left:

> *I am very much for the development of non-state charities, relief agencies, orphanages, youth hostels, squats, shelters for battered women, the homeless or the mentally ill, self-improvement programs for drug addicts and alcoholics, assistance services for the disabled or the elderly, wildlife and environmental preserves, means of food and drug testing independent of the state bureaucracy, home schools, neighborhood schools, private schools, tenants organizations, mutual banks, credit unions, consumers unions, anarcho-syndicalist labor unions and other worker organizations, cooperatives, communes, collectives, kibbutzim and other alternative models of organizing*

production. I am in favor of free clinics, alternative medicine, self-diagnostic services, midwifery, the abolition of medical licensure, the repeal of prescription laws and anything else that could potentially reduce the cost of health care for the average person and diminish dependency on the medical-industrial complex and the white coat priesthood. Indeed, I would argue that the eventual success of libertarianism depends to a large degree on the ability of libertarians to develop workable alternatives to both the corporation-dominated economy and the state-dominated welfare and social service system. To the degree that libertarians fail to do so will be the degree to which we continue to be regarded as plutocratic apologists without concern for the unfortunate or downtrodden on the right end or as just another species of Chomskyite anarcho-social democrats on the left end.

The student protests of Paris, May 1968 brought on a whole new approach to left struggles that were outside of the state and labor movement (and I believe now define the new left).

No doubt about it. Yet a core element of my arguments is that the New Left of 1968 is now the status quo.

This will all be explained in more detail later, the point being that it is overwhelmingly easy to glean that Anarchists have always been opposed to forms of authority outside of the state until the right retro-actively tried to place themselves in-line with the leftist thinkers of the past.

This ignores the fact that the American right is historically rooted in the left (e.g classical liberalism) and that many right-wing movements in the Anglosphere today reflect this classical liberal influence, e.g. libertarianism, paleoconservatism, populism, Anabaptist influenced forms of Christian evangelicalism, or agrarianism. Moreover, the ideas of the radical traditionalists that have influenced a number of Third Positionist tendencies overlap very well with those of classical anarchists. The radical traditionalist journal *Tyr* describes its principles as "*resacralization of the world versus materialism, natural social hierarchy versus an artificial hierarchy based on wealth, the tribal community versus the nation-state, stewardship of the earth versus the maximization of resources, a harmonious relationship between men and women versus the war between the sexes, and handicraft and artisanship versus industrial mass-production.*"

This vision sounds almost Kropotkinite, does it not?

Moreover, Preston has stated that he accepts:

"natural inequality of persons at both the individual and collective levels, the inevitability and legitimacy of otherness"

This places, at least, Preston himself in the position of the conservative thesis, the sociological side generally associated with the right, if not Third Positionism itself. If nothing else, it distances the entire notion of Third Positionism from Anarchism and the classical understanding of Libertarianism outside of the US. It is ideologically impossible to claim any lineage to Anarchist thought without the idea that social inequality is to some extent a social construct.

Where have I ever denied that "social inequality is to some extent a social construct"? Do the English and the Afghans have "equal" levels of social evolution concerning gender relations? Would not the relationship between the culture of the Dutch and that of the Saudis constitute an inevitable "otherness"? Equus next turns his attention to the question of the state itself.

There is no doubt that old leftist ideas have gained popularity amongst western industrialized states. Public education and universal healthcare are just two examples of leftist ideas practiced by the state.

No doubt about it. But is this a good thing? The traditional anarchist critique of state-controlled education is that it is a means of disseminating the state's legitimating ideology and inculcating youngsters with pious reverence for the state. The historic purpose of the welfare state was the cooptation, pacification, and subjugation of peoples' movements by making people dependent on the state and crowding out alternatives. Kevin Carson has written extensively of the progressive welfare state's efforts to overrun popular institutions, and the welfare state idea has its roots in Prussian militarism. An anarchist who cannot grasp these principles is not worthy of the name.

This does not, however, place leftism firmly in the statist sphere of political belief. The Left, like the Right, has statist and anti-statist strands of thought. However, it is also true that the Left has significant, even dominant, strands of extreme statist tendencies exhibited in such movements as Jacobinism, Marxism, and Leninism.

National Socialism, a clearly right-wing ideology, has seen itself manifested in the state.

Well, the true origins of National Socialism are something of an embarrassment to the Left.

Most leftists, adhering to the conflict theorist understanding of social inequality, believe that the state is a tool that can be used to minimize or destroy social inequality,

This simply means that "most leftists" are incompatible with Anarchism.

Similarly, most of the right sees the state as a way to ensure that a system of stratification is as functional as possible,

The pro-state Right is likewise incompatible with Anarchism. Thus it does not mean the anti-state Right should be shunned.

The New Left is intensely critical of authoritarian statism (as Paris 1968 demonstrated), but does not leave behind old understandings of authority (class oppression, gender oppression, racism, etc.).

This statement completely ignores what the New Left has subsequently evolved into, and the fact that the New Left has become part of the status quo.

On the State, Anarchism, Goals, and Strategies

A key objection Equus raises against my position involves the contention that left and right wing anti-statists, whatever their surface appearances, oppose the state for fundamentally different, even diametrically opposed, and therefore incompatible reasons.

If nothing else, Third Positionism does not lay in the same historical bed as Anarchism, it's not even in the same bedroom. While there may be right-wing thinkers that see the state as a mechanism to ensure the functionality of a society and others who see it as a roadblock, neither the left or right necessarily see it as a tool that must be used. Without the understanding that social stratification is to some extent socially constructed, Third Positionism and ATS are squarely on the right of the ongoing political discourse, accepting that social inequality is inevitable.

First of all, not all Third Positionists are necessarily anti-statists, and those who are will more likely be decentralists of some kind or merely interested in pan-secessionism as a tactic, rather than adhering specifically to branches of anarchism that are directly influenced by Third Positionist thinking (like national-anarchism). In terms of forming alliances with third position-influenced groups, I would say "take them as they come," meaning evaluate specific groups and individuals on the basis of what they can or could likely contribute to a wider anarcho-pluralist movement employing pan-secessionism as a tactic. Equus regards left and right wing anti-statists as incompatible on the basis of perceived differences in their respective understandings of human nature, particularly their contending views on "inequality." While the elitism/egalitarianism dichotomy is not as picture perfect as Equus would have us believe, even if we concede this point for the sake of argument, it still does not follow that left and right wing anti-statists have no common ground. Equus goes on to describe a laundry list of points of view that should be excluded from the anarchist movement.

> *This does not exclude Market Anarchists or Individualist Anarchists from the Anarchist movement (although it most certainly does exclude "Anarcho-capitalists"). The market, like the state, is a tool, a forum, a method. It is a tool by which Anarchists seek freedom from hierarchy and those on the right use to legitimize it. The Anarchist would claim, "The market will liberate all individuals from hierarchy," while only the rightist would claim, "Any hierarchy as a result of the market is legitimate, fair, or natural and must be accepted since it is a result of the market." **The left seeks to reform or destroy hierarchy; the right seeks to legitimize it.** The tools they use depend on the individuals.*

These are just word games. Why should anarcho-capitalists be excluded from the anarchist movement? Surely, we would want to exclude *state*-capitalists. I agree there is no room for plutocratic "conservatives" or vulgar "libertarians" in our ranks. But there is no reason why those who want to set up economic arrangements involving a Lockean basis for property rights or voluntarily employing wage labor should be prohibited from doing so in a stateless system.

> *The reason Third Positionism, the populist right in the USA, and other right-wing ideologies have recently become anti-state or at least garner harsh feelings toward the idea of government is easily understandable in a historical context. It is a relatively new phenomenon from my understanding that the right can be*

associated with anti-state sentiment at all. As the left gained support in the government via the labor movement, black power movement, feminist movement, etc. the government has adopted some ideas from the left while maintaining social stratification. Public education and healthcare are two examples of this.

This amounts to an admission by Equus that the Left has indeed become part of the status quo in many, many areas of society.

In this sense, the right is opposed to government because the government has adopted ideas that are diametrically opposed to its traditional beliefs.

Yes, in some instances, but so what? Naturally, in an anti-state movement some people will oppose the state out of consistent hostility to the state, while others will oppose it only because they see it as antithetical to their own interests.

Inasmuch as the right opposes the current trend of governments, the alliance between Anarchists and the "libertarian" right is faulty at least, and most likely hazardous. ATS' Statement of Purpose legitimizes and says it accepts the following schools of thought:

"anarcho-monarchism, anarcho-feudalism"

Being that some of the first Anarchist thinkers, let's just use Proudhon and Baukunin as examples, lived in societies that had feudal, monarchist states it becomes increasingly hard, and as any further thought will prove impossible, to reconcile the term "anarcho-monarchism." If Anarchism as a philosophy was first articulated in the face of Monarchist/feudal systems, how then could it have progressed towards them? Without retroactive defining that is completely delineated from Anarchism, it is impossible to give anarcho-monarchism any credibility.

Once again, a distinction must be made between *state*-monarchism or *state*-feudalism and anarcho-monarchism and anarcho-feudalism, just as a distinction has to be made between state-capitalism and anarcho-capitalism, state-communism and anarcho-communism, or state-syndicalism and anarcho-syndicalism. Clearly, an anarcho-communist commune such as Twin Oaks is the polar opposite of state-communist regimes such as North Korea, Cuba, or the former Soviet Union. Clearly, a syndicalist model workers' cooperative federation such as Mondragon is the polar opposite of the state-corporatist "syndicalism" of Mussolini. Clearly, a purely private business firm employing voluntary wage labor is the polar opposite of state-capitalist entities such as General Motors. Likewise, an anarcho-monarchist community where the participants voluntarily appoint a monarch or a collection of monarchs to serve such functions as the organization of protection or settling disputes is the polar opposite of the absolute monarchies championed by Thomas Hobbes. Prototypes for anarcho-monarchist societies can be found throughout history and contemporary Liechtenstein comes close to being such an arrangement. Likewise, it is possible that, for instance, an anarchist seastead or colony might voluntarily anoint certain individuals to be dukes, barons, counts, knights, and so forth, thereby setting up a kind of anarcho-feudalism. Indeed, "anarcho-feudalism" might well be conceptually useful in those countries where feudal titles still carry some influence, and where common people maintain a sacralized vision of the process whereby those titles are issued. Further, it is possible that in an anarcho-pluralist pan-secessionist action that some regions or localities of a more conservative bent might be inclined towards anarcho-capitalism, anarcho-monarchism, or anarcho-feudalism, while those of a more liberal or progressive bent might be inclined towards anarcho-syndicalism, anarcho-communism, or mutualist anarchism. Others may think what they wish of such beliefs or actions, but the disapproval of others does not invalidate their legitimacy.

Equus goes on to make a number of comments, with the same assertions repeated to the point of redundancy, concerning the history of private violence between left and right wing extremists. The following is a sufficient illustration of such comments:

> However (and what an ominous word that can be!), when the "matters of controversy" are ideologies, or, people supporting and espousing ideologies that are diametrically opposed to those held by Anarchists it becomes an entirely different matter. It is simply illogical to fight alongside someone who may very well want to murder, beat, or rape you post-revolution. Perhaps the words "murder," "beat," and "rape" seem extreme, but they most certainly are not, especially when one places "Anarcho-nationalism" in-line with Anarchism. Nationalists across Europe, and fascists all over, have indeed murdered, raped, and beaten Anarchists throughout history inside and outside of the state.

I might be inclined to take such sentiments seriously if it were not for the fact that the so-called "anti-fascists" have a lengthy history of collaboration with Communist groups, whose tendency towards bloody repression of anarchists once in power is well-known. Besides, it is ludicrous to associate all rightist political activity with violent neo-Nazi psychopaths, and so-called "anti-fascists" are not beyond engaging in unprovoked criminal violence of their own. Suffice to say that in a libertarian legal order, aggressive violence (whether by "fascists" or "anti-fascists") would be disallowed.

> *The idea behind Third Positionism is that two communities that oppose each other will not live together and go on to their respective communities post secession, but assume for a moment that these two hypothetical groups live in the same neighborhood. By the "anarcho-nationalist" point of view, if that neighborhood is rightfully theirs (say the majority of the neighborhood is anti-Semitic) then there is absolutely nothing to stop them from murdering, raping, and/or beating their Jewish neighbor.*

The inclination towards aggressive violence is hardly something that is unique only to "fascists." The possibility of intercommunal violence following the breakdown of the state is all the more reason to build a pan-secessionist movement that works towards negotiated alliances and settlements for the purpose of avoiding such violence.

> *Say there is a Tibetan Anarchist who was dropped off at this Monastery as a child. He/she now identifies with the community he/she lives in, but cannot help his belief that the organization of the monastery is wrong. He/she talks about it with some friends and they all agree. Soon, there's a faction of Buddhist monks that wish to reform the organization of their monastery. Does an Anarchist across the planet now turn the same indifferent eye towards the monastery?*

> *Hell no.*

This is the psychology of a Christian missionary who cannot bear the idea that even one soul in the far corners of the earth might not achieve salvation. Having been both a Christian fundamentalist and a reactionary leftist at various points in my life, all I can say is that I'm done with trying to save the world. Others may attempt to do so if they wish.

Nowhere in Equus' rebuttal does he outline any provisions for what his ideal form of anarchism might look like, nor does he discuss any ideas on how such preferences might be achieved. This statement by Equus is indicative of what is wrong with left-wing anarchism at present:

> *Since Anarchists (leftists) all have a general consensus about what they are against and the only legitimate quibbles are about what they are for, there is no real reason to call for a broad alliance of them since it already exists.*

In other words, left-wing anarchism is simply a reactionary movement with a laundry list of what it opposes. It offers no practical vision of what is it for because it doesn't have one. Like the Marxists, the presumption of the left-anarchists is that all will be fine once the state simply withers away. Historical experience reveals this to be foolishness. I realized as much twenty years ago, which is why I went on to found American Revolutionary Vanguard and AttacktheSystem.Com for the purpose of building an alternative anarchist movement that is devoid of such weaknesses. Our own tendencies are growing exponentially, and expanding to an increasingly diverse array of demographic groups. Likewise, our preferred tactic of pan-secessionism continues to receive conventional media coverage. We are the future of anarchism, and not those who are stuck in a time warp where it is always 1968.

15

No Friends to the Right, No Enemies to the Left?

An article by Spencer Sunshine, "Drawing the Lines Against Racism and Fascism," of Political Research Associates (led by "former" Stalinist Chip Berlet and funded by the Ford Foundation, representatives of the left-wing of capitalism) is well worth reading because it's an excellent illustration of the pathology, paranoia, and hypocrisy that dominates the particular strand of the hard left that "Sunshine" represents.

This guy is specifically arguing that "progressives" (whatever that means) should exclude from their midst not only the "far right" (presumably everything from moderate conservatives to Nazis) but also anyone from the left, libertarians, "people of color," presumably gays, LGBTs, etc. that do not tow the leftist party line, or who are judged guilty by association. Sunshine puts his cards on the table to a much greater degree than most leftists. This actually works to our advantage because he's allowing the "totalitarian humanists" to be seen for what they really are. The implicit racial arrogance of white leftism is also exposed. This guy is essentially taking it upon himself to decide how minorities should go about being minorities, and what is an appropriate range or mode of thought for "people of color." This is standard white leftist racial paternalism.

I've always found the racism of these hard left types to be rather astounding. I first noticed it when I was part of the hard left years ago, and it's become much more obvious with time. They vacillate between viewing minorities as children who need rescuing, as weaklings who can't do anything for themselves, or as pawns to be used as tools of the "revolution." Nothing pisses them off more than a minority that doesn't play the leftist game. Such a person immediately becomes a "self-hater," "Uncle Tom," "opportunist," "sell out," etc. The racist tradition within the context of the historic US racial caste system was for white supremacists to regard a self-assertive or independently minded non-white person as an "uppity n——" who "doesn't know his place." I see that kind of attitude on the Left as well, although it's masked behind a humanitarian or egalitarian charade. Also, Sunshine's lack of any sincere or principled anti-authoritarian values is demonstrated by his failure to exclude totalitarian leftists from "progressive" circles such as the pro-North Korean Workers World Party, the Maoist Revolutionary Communist Party (allies of the Pol Potist Sendoro Luminoso), the Trotskyist Socialist Workers Party, Spartacist League, or International Socialist Organization (disciples of the chief perpetrator of Krondstadt), etc., etc., etc. He even mentions his inclusive attitude towards "liberal Democrats" (the ruling party of the mother country of the empire, and the only party to ever use nuclear weapons in war).

If this kind of thinking is explicitly adopted by the more reactionary sectors of the Left, it will work to our advantage because it will leave large sectors of well-meaning anti-system people who would otherwise be drawn to the Left without a political home. Meanwhile, we will be there to welcome them.

Some of this stuff is funny. This passage here sounds like Bob Larson raving about Satanic rock in the 80s:

> "Progressive groups should come up with their own criteria for people who want to move away from Far Right politics and toward progressive political communities. Recommendations for this include: 1) requiring the person make a public statement disavowing Far Right views, and posting it in their former group's media; 2) turning over all Far Right books, t-shirts, buttons, etc. to antifascists— especially patches or other insignia of any organizations they were members of; 3) removing all Far Right contacts on social media, and not attending events (either social, cultural, or political) hosted by these individuals or groups; 4) making a sincere statement of why their former views were problematic, with apologies made to anyone hurt by their actions. (The letter written by former White nationalist Derek Black, son of Stormfront founder Don Black, is exemplary.) If they want to become actively involved as progressive political organizers, they should also 5) be required to go through a debrief to provide information about their former Rightist group's structures, membership, recruiting tactics, and beliefs."

Another funny part is his repeated assertion that when "far right" groups have "people of color" among their members, well, that only goes to show how deceitfully racist they are.

The Tyranny of the Politically Correct

Perhaps Spencer Sunshine is really some kind of right-wing undercover operative whose real goal is to undermine the Left by making it as boring as possible. Kids in particular like to join radical movements for excitement, adventure, and rebellion, and not to be lectured to by a bunch of dour puritans.

I was at a libertarian-anarchist conference in Acapulco a couple of weeks ago, and one thing I realized while I was there is just how big anti-system currents outside this reactionary left nonsense are getting to be, from the various strands of the radical right to libertarians to *Russia Today*-style leftists to the conspiracy milieu to leftists, progressives, anarchists, minorities, gays, etc., who are tired of these overbearing politically correct left-fascists/neo-Stalinists. A whole new wave of radical political undercurrents is growing from the bottom up and eventually these left-fascist assholes are going to be overrun. I suspect we will see a lot more anti-System people coming our way in the future as more and more leftists become frustrated with the basket case state of the Left.

We've got guys like Spencer Sunshine out there doing their part to make it known we exist, and likely driving plenty of people towards us with their attitude. I'm increasingly getting messages from leftists saying things like, "I used to think you were a scumbag, but I'm coming around to your position more and more."

In more recent times, I've noticed that the Left really is starting to implode due to the constant fighting among the rival PC factions over who is most oppressed and all that. The left-anarchists, for example, can hardly even have public gatherings anymore without physical altercations breaking out. I'm talking about fistfights between the transgendered and feminists, or between vegans and vegetarians, or other comparable instances of lunacy. The reason they hate us isn't merely because we blur the left/right distinction, or because they think we're fascists. These people all hate each other, and I think it's reflective of their psychological makeup as much as anything else. The social left in its present form attracts a lot of psychologically damaged and pathological people, and fringe politics provides them with a forum for acting out.

It might also be helpful to identify fault lines on the Left we can use to our advantage. Exposing the establishment connections and funding of the "watchdogs" would be one of these. So would providing an alternative forum for people on the Left who are tired of the crap, and are interested in finding new ways, thereby encouraging mass defections from the Left. Another might be to create rifts between these left-fascist/neo-Stalinist factions by hammering away at the fact that they're basically a mixture of anarcho-communists, Stalinists, and Trots, and persistently pointing out the history of bloodshed between these groups.

The main thing the totalitarian Left is afraid of is our ability to "take the game away" from them. Matthew Lyons has said that repeatedly, for example. They know that tendencies like ours offer a very open ended paradigm that is able to move past the usual barriers of left and right, uniting all kinds of anarchists and other radicals, members of different racial and religious groups, adherents of different economic philosophies, etc. against the System. This is terrifying to both establishment leftists like the SPLC, who seek to advance themselves within the context of the system, and the hard leftists, who envision some kind of totalitarian revolution led and controlled by themselves, or for whom participation in radical politics is simply a manifestation of personal pathologies.

16

More Anarchistic Than Thou

An uninformed lay person reading the pathetically ignorant and barely literate bromide against Attack the System recently issued by "Anti-Fascist News" would hardly know anarchism is a vast tradition in modern political philosophy with roots in the radical Enlightenment more than two centuries ago. Further, history provides examples of many anarchist prototypes extending back for thousands of years (Peter Marshall's magisterial work "Demanding the Impossible" ably demonstrates this point). However, our critics at "Anti-Fascist News" would have everyone believe that the sum total of anarchist traditions have never been more than a sectarian brand of anarcho-communism derived from the left-wing of anarchism as it was in the 1930s. This is akin to a modern Protestant fundamentalist insisting that the entire Christian tradition consists of nothing more than seventeenth century English Puritanism (no offense to Puritans).

While I am an admirer of the anarcho-communist tendency within classical anarchism of the early twentieth century, there is certainly no reason why anarchism should be exclusively and forever defined within the confines of these limited parameters. As a reading of even the most elementary level book on anarchism will indicate, anarchism is in fact a collection of many varied and diverse currents just as (using the Christian analogy once again) the Christian faith consists of many thousands of traditions, sects, and denominations that have existed throughout history and throughout the world today. As John Zube has ably demonstrated, there are indeed many readily identifiable traditions within anarchism, some of which maintain a paradoxical relationship to each other. Of course, it is true that there will always likely remain sects within anarchism that refuse to recognize one another as "true" anarchists, just as there are sects of Protestants and Catholics, Sunni and Shiites, who refuse to recognize each other as "true" Christians or Muslims.

However, among the focuses of Attack the System is the creation of a kind of meta-politics that recognizes and aims to synthesize many varied currents within anarchist, libertarian, anti-statist, decentralist, anti-authoritarian, anti-capitalist, and anti-imperialist traditions in a way that aims to establish a new meta-ideological and meta-strategic paradigm that is capable of serving as an antithesis to the universal hegemony of global capitalist monoculture. Such a project necessarily involves transcending ordinary divisions of the kind that normally define the conventional Left and Right. A corollary to this effort is the recognition that different tendencies present divergent narratives that maintain their own appropriateness within their particular contexts. In other words, different forms of anarchism and overlapping philosophies present ideas that are relevant to particular people involved with specific struggles within the context of their own circumstances.

For example, it is entirely appropriate that anarcho-syndicalists are primarily interested in issues that pertain to workers, anarcho-feminists in issues that pertain to feminists, queer-anarchists in issues that pertain to queers, anarcho-pacifists in issues pertaining to resistance to militarism, black anarchists in issues pertaining to African-Americans, and eco-anarchists in issues that pertain to environmentalists. The wider pan-anarchist meta-political paradigm favored by Attack the System certainly does not insist that any particular hyphenated tendency, subterranean ideological strand :-) or sub-tendency renounce its preferred economic system, identity orientation, or favorite social cause. However, the position of Attack the System is that anarchism should not be limited to a focus on issues that are generally favored by leftists. For example, anarchists should not merely focus on demographic conflict within particular societies. As I have written elsewhere:

> On this question, the radical left typically puts the cart before the horse. It is well and good to defend unpopular minorities against genuine oppression and to agitate for the ongoing expansion of civil liberties. But it is strategically foolish to adopt an antagonistic stance towards the traditional and majoritarian culture of the working masses by attempting to pit varying demographic groups against one another in the form of blacks against whites, women against men, gays against straights, immigrants against natives, tree-huggers against loggers, animal lovers against meat-eaters, eco-freaks against small property owners, peace creeps against veterans, hippies against blue collar workers, poor Appalachian whites against Jewish bankers or whatever.

Instead, a more holistic and meta-political approach would involve a wider geopolitical outlook that was perhaps primarily related to formulating analyses of, for example, conflicts between American imperialism the various global opposition forces (BRICS, Resistance Block, resistance nations in Latin America, "rogue states," non-state actors), between liberal European civilization and conservative Islamic civilization, between the East and West, and between the Global North and the Global South. Likewise, when examining the internal politics of individual states it might be appropriate to examine ways in which statism and corporatism engage in oppression and exploitation across conventional boundaries of class, race, gender, region, cultural identity, and so forth.

It is also necessary to criticize leftist as well as rightist forms of political authoritarianism. Indeed, the tradition of leftist authoritarianism extends as far back as the legacy of the Jacobins of the French Revolution, and extends through the entire history of the First International, the Russian Revolution, the Spanish Civil War, and so on. A mere three decades ago, more than a third of the world's population lived under explicitly leftist dictatorships, and these dictatorships are widely recognized by historians as having been among the most genocidal and democidal in history, with the number of casualties they inflicted perhaps totaling as high as 100 million. Yet we see no mention of this in the screed issued by "Anti-Fascist News" when their hysterical references to "genocide" appear. And, in fact, it is also true that many so-called "anti-fascists" explicitly identify as Communists, and at times utilize a hammer and sickle as an insignia. Therefore, the claims of the "anti-fascists" to be principled opponents of oppression by totalitarian states is not to be taken seriously, but merely regarded as a form of reactionary leftist opportunism.

A wide range of issues also exist that should reasonably be of interest to anarchists besides those issues that normally appeal to leftists (such as "racism, sexism, and homophobia"). For example, why are anarchists not actively involved in the defense of the right to keep and bear arms? Indeed, anarchists should be joining the National Rifle Association and the Gun Owners of America and seeking leadership positions in such organizations. Why are anarchists not supporting the home school movement, organized tax resistance, issues related to local sovereignty, opposition to compulsory education, the interests of small farmers and the self-employed, resistance to classist zoning regulations, alternative medicine, and a wide range of other anti-statist, anti-corporate issues that fall outside of the leftist paradigm? Above all, why are anarchists not actively working to defend the freedoms of

143

speech, association, and religion, due process, academic freedom, and scientific inquiry that are among the most fundamental achievements of modern societies? These have been persistently subject to attack in the name of ostensibly "progressive" political correctness, and not a few anarchists have been profoundly complicit in this.

Of course, what the "anti-fascists" seem to object to the most is the position maintained by Attack the System that identity politics formulated by groups that are disfavored by leftists are legitimate. Attack the System does not oppose the maintenance of identity politics by African-Americans, Native-Americans, Hispanic-Americans, Arab-Americans, Asian-Americans, Jews, Muslims, Buddhists, Hindus, Wiccans, the LGBTQ umbrella, feminists, atheists, vegetarians, vegans, immigrants, environmentalists, the elderly, young people, disabled people, fat people, ugly people, students, gamers, drug users, sex workers, slut walkers, street gangs, prison inmates, or Star Wars fans. Likewise, Attack the System does not oppose the maintenance of identity politics by Protestant evangelicals, Catholic traditionalists, adherents of Eastern Orthodoxy, Mormons, Europeans, Caucasian-Americans, Southerners, Midwesterners, Catalans, Scots, Basques, Russians, Englishmen, Irishmen, Scientologists, Moonies, the white working class, WASPs, yuppies, men, social conservatives, cultural traditionalists, ethnic preservationists, Euro-pagan tribalists, gun owners, meat eaters, tobacco smokers, rednecks, military veterans, motorcycle gangs, survivalists, metal heads, or aficionados of classical music.

The most common objection that is raised to this perspective by the Left is the claim that many in the former category of social groups represents oppressed or subordinated classes of people, while many in the latter category represents hegemonic or "privileged" categories. Obviously, there is a considerable degree of truth to some of these claims in a historical sense, depending on the group in question and the specific historical context, but such claims are increasingly dubious within the context of contemporary demographic, cultural, generational, socioeconomic, and political realities. Sorry folks, but Barack Obama's America is not the America of Dwight Eisenhower or even Ronald Reagan, let alone Andrew Jackson, and this will be increasingly true in the years and decades ahead, particularly as WASPs lose their historic demographic majority in the United States, and become just another minority group like everyone else (and therefore reasonably entitled to an identity politics of their own).

Lastly, there is the need for anarchists to think strategically. The ambition of Attack the System is to forge a society-wide pan-decentralist consensus, and this means appealing to the entire range of cultural and ideological currents that hold some degree of interest in such concepts, whether out of conviction or for tactical purposes. While such a perspective would certainly be of benefit to more "conservative" social sectors that desire separation from the wider liberal paradigm, it would also be of benefit to honest leftists that are genuinely seeking to overthrow the present imperialist plutocratic regime, as I have written elsewhere, and to minorities that are genuinely seeking self-determination (by, for example, ridding their communities of racist occupational police forces and adopting a system of self-policing). And the primary beneficiaries of the overthrow of the American empire, the principal ambition of Attack the System, would be the millions of people around the world that are threatened with slaughter by the empire that Attack the System has identified as its primary enemy.

As for some of the sillier claims made by "Anti-Fascist News":

> *"Literally, every single traditional anarchist that Preston likes to prop up on his website, Attack the System, consider themselves primarily of an anti-capitalist tradition. Emma Goldman, Alexander Berkman, Mikhail Bakunin, Peter Kropotkin, and even Pierre Joseph Proudhon and Max Stirner, were all violently anti-capitalist."*

It is unclear where the claims that Attack the System is a "pro-capitalist" tendency originate from. This is interesting considering that many conventional conservatives and libertarian-capitalists consider us to be socialists or even Marxists. Attack the System is not a tendency that is primarily oriented towards economic issues, and a variety of economic perspectives are included under the ATS umbrella. My own economic views are fairly similar to those of Kevin Carson, Will Schnack, or Larry Gambone (I also agree with Gambone's assessment of Rothbard), and I even wrote an award-winning article some years ago attacking corporate plutocracy.

> *"While many traditions have split from the surface political forms of this, the foundational ideas have remained the same. Rudolph Rocker brought these ideas into the workplace, Emma Goldman elaborated them into gender and sexual liberation, and as they came up through the 20th century they adapted to the struggles against oppression from different oppressed identities...*

145

Anarchism, at its core, has always been an idea about the smashing of social and political hierarchy, embedded in capitalism and enforced by the state. It is not that anarchists are opposed to the state just because it is a bureaucratic machine, but instead because it enforces ruling class interests and are created in the image of that class. To be opposed to the state is because of its role in capitalism, patriarchy, and white supremacy. There is literally no connection then to "national anarchist" ideas that are based around the idea that white people are somehow an oppressed class, which is against all common understanding of power and history. There is no role for bigotry, anti-Semitism, the oppression of women and queer people, or for the rich to maintain their wealth..."

There was plenty of political incorrectness among classical anarchists. The anti-Semitism of Proudhon, Bakunin, and Duhring, the anti-feminism of Proudhon and Most, the homophobia within Spanish anarchism, the support of Kropotkin, Tucker, and Faure for World War One, Rocker's later support for the Cold War, the Christianity of Tolstoy, the conservative Catholicism of Dorothy Day, Goldman's Nietzscheanism and skepticism of women's suffrage, Landauer's folkish nationalism and Bavarian regionalism, the support of West Coast tendencies within the IWW for the Chinese Exclusion movement, Proudhon's French patriotism and sympathetic view of racism in the Western hemisphere, Bakunin's pan-Slavic nationalism, the nationalist orientation of the massive Chinese anarchist movement of the early twentieth century, and Kropotkin's apparent admiration of Mussolini, are just a few examples. It is not that any of these were necessarily good ideas, but are instead illustrations that the anarchist tradition is not as untainted according to contemporary PC standards as "*Anti-Fascist News*" would seemingly claim. But the point is that many of the luminaries of historic anarchism might well have felt quite at home at the National Policy Institute or the H.L. Mencken Club.

"In a recent presentation at NPI, Preston embarrassed himself as he went on to show how white nationalism was compatible with anarchism..."

"...he spit out his idea of "totalitarian humanism," which is one of his charming notions that the left forces their ideology of "humanism" on the right. His use of these types of labels is a way of creating a mirage about the fact that he is playing with pre-school ideas about how the world works, where by any attempt to confront racism and domination is somehow the real oppression. To do

146

this it doesn't require any deeper analysis about white supremacy, heteronormativity, or what people of oppressed classes have actually experienced in their lives. Instead, Preston can rail against Political Correctness as the true evil, which I'm sure is much worse than the crisis of sexual assault happening against women worldwide or the vicious cruelty of de-regulated capitalism on the working class."

Oh, cry me a river of crocodile tears. I have thoroughly documented how what I call "totalitarian humanism" is the self-legitimating ideological superstructure of contemporary Western liberal democratic capitalist regimes. In trying to trace the origins of PC, it seems to represent the convergence and cumulative effect of a range of historical, cultural, and ideological forces. There is the legacy of Christian "slave morality" (see Nietzsche), Protestant pietism and Puritanism (see Rothbard), Enlightenment universalism and egalitarianism, Marxist eschatology and dualism, progressive Christian revisionism (the "social gospel," see Paul Gottfried), critical theory (see Lind on the Frankfurt School), Gramscianism, black Marxism (DuBois), American Stalinism (Allen and Ignatiev), Western Maoism (Weather Underground), a general backlash against the legacy of European colonialism, the American and South African racial caste systems, and Nazism, WW2, and the Holocaust, the growth of therapeutic, consumer culture within the context of a post-scarcity managerial society, and the rise of a left-wing capitalist class from outside of the traditional Western elites, which includes the newly rich generated by newer high-tech industries (like media and computers), the coming to power of elites among traditional outgroups (racial minorities, women, homosexuals), and the hijacking of all of these by the state as a means of creating a self-legitimating ideological superstructure and moralistic posture to mask imperial hegemony (see Chomsky on "military humanism") in the tradition of liberal imperialism. But the most important point for anarchists is that totalitarian humanism, at least in its more extreme manifestations, is simply the latest trend in left-wing authoritarianism, in the tradition of Jacobinism, Blanquism, Marxism, Leninism, Stalinism, and Maoism.

"In Preston's most recent book, named Attack the System, after his own website, he put a big American flag on the cover alongside a few bullets. Do you think that anarchism is unique to America as a country? Do you think that the imperial state of the U.S., built on slavery and exploitation, and crystalized in the flag, is somehow anarchist? What do you think most anarchists would see when they see your claims of a "new anarchist perspective" emblazoned in front of the American flag?"

147

It takes a special kind of mind to accuse me, of all people, of an excess of patriotism or of being an apologist for American imperialism. Ironically, my book is about as "anti-American" as they come. Noam Chomsky looks like a flag waving "USA! USA!" jingoist compared to me. In fact, the actual subject of my most recent presentation at the National Policy Institute was a comprehensive critique of American imperialism. Indeed, I have found that it is on the "far right" of domestic American politics where an "anti-American" analysis of international geopolitical relations is the most welcome.

The bottom line is that the task of revolutionary struggle against the state, the global plutocratic super class, and the Empire is far too important and too challenging to be placed in the hands of recycled Commies and over privileged undergraduates hiding away in their "safe spaces" with their crayons and coloring books, desperately seeking to avoid being "triggered," and crying over this or that "microaggression." However, the many traditions within anarchism continue to offer much of value with regards to political theory, economics, ecology, social criticism, organizational methods, styles of activism, and the like. It is not the philosophy of anarchism but the character and competence of many present day anarchists that is sorely in need of revision.

17

Ignoring the Elephant in the Room

The bulk of AFN's latest screed against ATS is merely a diatribe against anarcho-capitalism and national-anarchism. It's odd is that so much energy would be devoted to an attack on anarcho-capitalism, which is a position I don't personally hold to, and we've had plenty of articles, including feature material, posted on ATS criticizing anarcho-capitalists and orthodox right-libertarians. We do have Rothbardians and other an-caps that have written for us as well. But that's hardly a principal focus of ATS. There are plenty of right-libertarians and conventional "free market conservatives" who consider us to be Marxists. I even wrote an award-winning essay some years ago taking orthodox right-libertarians to task. Anarcho-capitalists are a mixed bag. Some are just good Lysander Spooner/Benjamin Tucker individualist-anarchists at heart. Some are really just mutualists or agorists. But others are Ayn Rand-loving corporate apologists. As is sometimes said, take what you can use and discard the rest.

AFN offers a similar tirade against national-anarchism, but offers little in the way of substance with regards to actually critiquing N-A. Instead, AFN merely regurgitates Spencer Sunshine's (not "Sam" Sunshine, at least get the name of authors you are quoting right, for god's sake) conspiracy theory about N-A supposedly being some kind of neo-Nazi subterfuge contrived for the purpose of taking over the anarchist movement. It's not exactly clear why neo-Nazis would even want to do such a thing given that neo-Nazis are trailed only by left-wing anarchism as the least influential ideologies on the political horizon.

To repeat the points I made in my earlier reply.

ATS exists to forge a pan-anarchist consensus for the purpose of developing a more effective united revolutionary front against the state. In this regard, ATS is merely a continuation of similar tendencies from the past like synthesist-anarchism or anarchism-without-adjectives.

Pan-secessionism is a tactical concept and strategic position, not an ideology. The ambition is to develop a consensus among all decentralist political tendencies towards the development of a popular front against the premiere institutions of international capitalism, such as the American federal government, American imperialism, the Anglo-American-Zionist-Wahhabist axis (the dominant wing of the international power elite), the European Union, and what Michael Hardt and Antonio Negri referred to as the "Empire," an international capitalist agglomeration centered around global financial and political institutions such as the World Trade Organization, International Monetary Fund, World Bank, United Nations, and various appendages. Pan-secessionism could be compared to older anarchist tactical concepts like the notion of the general strike.

ATS also favors the development of a society-wide pan-decentralist consensus as a practical alternative to imperialism, centralism, statism, and plutocracy. Hence, the emphasis on culturally diverse localized polities. A pan-anarchist organized pan-secessionist action for the purpose of achieving pan-decentralism would not look like the Tea Parties, the Mormon Church, or the National Rifle Association, nor would it look like Occupy Wall Street, GLAAD, or Black Lives Matter. What we promote at ATS is a concept that is over and above these kinds of cultural variances.

Regarding identity politics, AFN says:

> "The point here is that this identity means something in that the identity is a point of resistance to oppression, not identity for identity's sake. This "identity politics" (though it is clear he does not understand what identity politics are and why most anarchists oppose them) is something that the radical right often highlights since they want to compare their "white nationalism" with "black nationalism" as if they are both equally movements towards racial identity and the advocacy of an ethnic identity. The difference is that black nationalism is a response to white oppression and an identity used only as a tool to resist that historic oppression. For white nationalists to say that they are the same project is to deny the fact that the purpose is fundamentally different. White nationalists seek to double down on their perceived identity, essentializing their racial characteristics. This is fundamentally a different project, for a different purpose, and a radically different politic. Preston goes on to identify feminists in his list, which he has to understand is not an "identity" as much as a movement to overhaul society and dethrone patriarchy. To list this as an "identity" is again a sign that he doesn't

clearly understand why identities are used in anti-oppression politics.

It is not that "identity" is something that the left wants to create dividing lines around, but instead, for some people, a piece of their lives through which they have been oppressed, and therefore need to create solidarity with others who share the same background of oppression. To say that white people are in the same boat as people of color in terms of racially defined oppression is offensive right from the start."

This statement completely ignores a central argument I made in my previous response.

The most common objection that is raised to this perspective by the Left is the claim that many in the former category of social groups represents oppressed or subordinated classes of people, while many in the latter category represents hegemonic or "privileged" categories. Obviously, there is a considerable degree of truth to some of these claims in a historical sense, depending on the group in question and the specific historical context, but such claims are increasingly dubious within the context of contemporary demographic, cultural, generational, socioeconomic, and political realities. Sorry folks, but Barack Obama's America is not the America of Dwight Eisenhower or even Ronald Reagan, let alone Andrew Jackson, and this will be increasingly true in the years and decades ahead, particularly as WASPs lose their historic demographic majority in the United States, and become just another minority group like everyone else (and therefore reasonably entitled to an identity politics of their own).

The Western civilization of 2015 is hardly the Western civilization of the nineteenth century or even the mid-twentieth century. The bottom line is that AFN has failed to update its ideology in order to recognize the nature contemporary Western liberal democratic capitalist societies as they actually are in their present manifestation. As I previously stated:

I have thoroughly documented how what I call "totalitarian humanism" is the self-legitimating ideological superstructure of contemporary Western liberal democratic capitalist regimes. In trying to trace the origins of PC, it seems to represent the convergence and cumulative effect of a range of historical, cultural, and ideological forces. There is the legacy of Christian "slave morality" (see Nietzsche), Protestant pietism and Puritanism (see Rothbard), Enlightenment universalism and egalitarianism, Marxist eschatology and dualism, progressive Christian revisionism (the "social gospel," see Paul Gottfried), critical theory (see Lind on the Frankfurt School), Gramscianism, black Marxism (DuBois), American Stalinism (Allen and Ignatiev), Western Maoism (Weather Underground), a general backlash against the legacy of European colonialism, the American and South African racial caste systems, and Nazism, WW2, and the Holocaust, the growth of therapeutic, consumer culture within the context of a post-scarcity managerial society, and the rise of a left-wing capitalist class from outside of the traditional Western elites, which includes the newly rich generated by newer high-tech industries (like media and computers), the coming to power of elites among traditional outgroups (racial minorities, women, homosexuals), and the hijacking of all of these by the state as a means of creating a self-legitimating ideological superstructure and moralistic posture to mask imperial hegemony (see Chomsky on "military humanism") in the tradition of liberal imperialism.

Let's take a look at some more claims from AFN.

"Preston often likes to cite obscure pseudo-anarchists from history, while ignoring ninety-five percent of anarchist history and theory."

What??? Proudhon, Bakunin, Kropotkin, Duhring, Spanish anarchism, Tucker, Faure, Rocker, Tolstoy, Day, Goldman, Landauer and the IWW are "obscure pseudo-anarchists from history"?

The best example of anarchist social organization existed in response to the rise of the Fallange fascist party in Catalonia, and were eventually crushed fighting for survival against the Catholic nationalists. Anarchists rose up as primary actors in fighting the fascist party machine in Italy, Romania, Austria, and Germany, all of which show the history of the radical right as being the direct inverse of anarchism and dedicated to its destruction. As you prance around the National Policy Institute and promote your Americanized pan-libertarianism, you are celebrating the forces that have been the historic enemy of the anarchist movement and who have murdered anarchists by the thousands.

Well, this is a rather interesting accusation given its source. What are the roots of the "antifa" anyway? As a friend states:

"The Antifascist Action the antifa claims as their legacy today

was originally a highly nationalist and authoritarian branch of the German Communist Party (KPD). It was the follower of the Rötkampfer Bund, the paramilitary branch of the KPD, which was banned in 1932 by the German government.

It would be pretty much the same as NA claiming the Swastika as a symbol for anarchism. The historic ignorance of the Antifa/AFA is pretty stunning, considering the nationalist and even 'anti-Semitic' (the KPD reached out to the same crowd as the NSDAP and thus used the same anti-Jewish sentiments) past of their symbol (the one "Anti-Fascist News" uses) and name."

Where exactly did the present day leftist-Marxist "anarchist" movement originate from? In the 60s and 70s, Communism was the general thrust of the radical left, and anarchists were considered a tiny, freakish sideshow. But during the 80s when it was becoming obvious that the Soviet Union was on its way to becoming a failed state, and that Communism was just another tyrannical bureaucracy, many Marxists started reinventing themselves as Anarchists. There was some of that in the 60s but I think this trend started to grow in a big way in the 80s, which was the time when I first became involved in left-anarchism. I remember a veteran leftist telling me at the time that Anarchism had finally surpassed Communism as the dominant ideology of "radial progressives." So it seems as though what happened is that as the PC Left that came out of the 60s with all of its privilege theory, critical theory, etc became increasingly institutionalized, a lot of these people started claiming the Anarchist label to differentiate themselves from Soviet-style Communism, even if they retained all of the underlying neo-Marxist presumptions. Hence, the failure of Communism meant that Marxists merely refashioned themselves as Anarchists.

I see the work of tendencies like ATS and NAM as a necessary corrective to anarchism having gotten off course due to Marxist infiltration. Also, ATS and NAM actually have a workable theory of anarchism based on decentralized, pluralistic, particularism that recognizes the legitimacy of identities such as ethnicity, culture, religion, nationality, race, language, history, tradition, regionalism, local community, in addition to preferred economic arrangements, abstract political ideologies, and sub-cultural variations. These are what most people identify with anyway rather than some kind of One World utopia or arcane economic theories that most people don't even understand.

Historically, there has been just as much repression of anarchists by authoritarian regimes and movements of the Left as there has been from the Right. I might take the "antifa" seriously when their anti-communism becomes as virulent as their "anti-fascism."

Preston himself now has zero connection to larger anarchist movements and seems to have been deemed persona non grata from all political arenas except the far-right.

The "far right" is presently the only milieu where a comprehensive critique of imperialism as it actually exists in its present form can be presented. The "center-right/center left" mainstream paradigm is fully committed to neo-liberalism. While strands of the "far left" profess opposition to imperialism and capitalism, the Left utterly fails to critique or even recognize neo-liberalism's legitimating ideological superstructure of totalitarian humanism because the bulk of the Left shares the same fundamental ideological and cultural presumptions as neo-liberalism on these questions such as globalism, multiculturalism, uncritical acceptance of mass immigration, therapeutic culture, the managerial state, victimology, "political correctness," and military humanism. It is forbidden to criticize many of these things on the "far left." In addition, the bulk of the "far left" has degenerated into outright silliness as demonstrated by its fixation on trigger warnings, safe spaces, so-called "call out culture," and the ongoing sectarian wars between feminists and the transgendered, transsexuals and transvestites, vegans and vegetarians, anti-anti-Semites and anti-Zionists, white anarchist youth and anarchist people of color, gender feminists and sex workers, anti-BDSM and pro-BDSM, gays and socially conservative immigrants, Muslims and feminists, etc. etc. etc. etc. In other words, the Left has become utterly worthless as any kind of authentic opposition force The "far right" is the only place where my own anti-imperialist, anti-capitalist, anti-statist, "anti-American," and anti-totalitarian humanist perspective can be heard at the present time.

Sorry folks, but that's how it is.

18

"Visions So Radically Different..."

"Anti-Fascist News" has generated another round. Here is my "response to response to response to response."

> "The exchange between anarchism and Marxism has been complex and ongoing, yet this idea that Marxism has infiltrated anarchism and that is why it has adopted socially left values is not just bizarre, it has a zero basis in fact. Today, Marxist factions, as small and scattered as they are, are continually a socially conservatizing force and several steps behind in these struggles. This has always been true in older periods of Marxism where struggle is centrally set on a united working class along economic lines, not along lines of other oppressed identification."

I would agree that the focus of the Left has shifted over the past half century from a focus on class-based politics of the kind found in traditional Marxism to a focus on cultural politics. No argument there.

> "The idea is then proposed by neo-fascists (sic) that the Frankfurt School completely reshaped all social struggles on every level so that anti-racism and anti-patriarchal struggles would supplement class struggle. The main purpose of this conspiracy theory is to create a narrative whereby it is actually Jewish philosophers that have started this process and, therefore, must be only done for Jewish domination."

I would agree that the influence of the Frankfurt School has been very important in the shaping of the modern Left, though I reject the "Jewish conspiracy" explanation for this, or the view that roots of PC can be fully explained by Marxist influences.

> "There are literally no Marxist academics or organizers that would agree with the radical right's estimation of Marxism as the driving force towards social progress through the Frankfurt School."

See Martin Jay's *The Dialectical Imagination*.

> *"The KPD, the failed German Revolution, and the position of racism within their party is a history that fails to have a connection to modern anti-fascist organizing since the dynamics of state allied communist parties is past, but it does actually show the degree to which Marxism fails to address issues like racism, patriarchy, and queer liberation.*
>
> *Ideologically, the anarchist project of modern times owes so little to Marxism in all the ways that most people understand Marxist theory. Marxism does not see the power dynamics that are central to interpersonally identified oppressions, such as race or gender, as foundational. Instead, economic relation act as the base to the larger superstructure by which other forms of oppression can rest alongside disparate pieces of culture. This runs counter to most contemporary anarchist's conception of oppression, where anything beyond class struggle would have to be secondary."*

And yet AFN seems to fall back on a "workerist" position which is arguably even more self-defeating that the normal "race/gender/gay" paradigm of the left-anarchists given that membership in unions is at an all-time low in the US (maybe AFN is not in the US), the transient nature of employment in a service industry-driven economy, and the fact that the few influential unions that are left are largely public sector unions whose employment interests are directly connected to the state.

> *"National Anarchism seeks to build up the idea of the ethnic nation as a viable unit of identity and resistance, but we want to counter that notion with the idea that working class unity and broad community is both more functionally successful in terms of struggle and more inspiring to the human soul."*

In the interests of clarity, I should point out that the argument I was making in my previous reply to "Anti-Fascist News" wasn't about taking anyone's side in the "Who's most oppressed?" pissing contest as much as it was to point out the limitations of the approach to political theory and social criticism offered by the contemporary Left.

"Anti-Fascist News" seems to represent a hybrid of sectarian 1930s model anarcho-communism ("workerism") and Communist-inspired "anti-fascist" movements from the same period. AFN hypocritically waxes hysterical about National-Anarchism, or supposed rightist influences on ATS, while glossing over the legacy of Communist repression of anarchists. In other words, AFN is engaged in special pleading, which is often the case with these hyper-leftist people.

"The influence of Marxism on anarchism is in much of the critiques of capitalism, which you would see in the work of people like Wayne Price (We are guessing you remember him)."

Yes, I am familiar with Wayne Price and his work.

"The Marxism that does tend to maintain some influence in anarchist circles are, ironically, by the Marxists that you cited to make your point. There is differing opinions about the work of Negri and Hardt among our editorial collective, especially as it comes to the de-emphasis of the nation state, yet this disagreement is within a particular framework: namely, the discussion of politics leading towards liberation. If anything, anarchism has influenced Marxism more on social issues than the latter as you can see the emergence in most of the ideas in many of the anarchists Preston sites, such as Alexander Berkman and Emma Goldman."

I am essentially a hard leftist at heart myself. I generally agree, for example, with the critique of the international capitalist system generated by globalization that Hardt and Negri outlined in "Empire," though I would argue that the Anglo-American-Zionist-Wahhabist axis is the dominant coalition within the "Empire." I generally agree with the "power elite" critique of domestic American politics offered by C. Wright Mills (plus the "four networks" modification of Mills' original theory offered by William Domhoff). However, I would argue that totalitarian humanism is the dominant coalition (with the left-wing of capitalism and the left-wing of the middle class being the dominant players on this coalition) within the U.S. system at present.

The problem with folks like AFN is that they are simply unable to recognize the degree to which the narrative of the cultural Left (privilege theory, critical theory, therapeutic culture, victimology, anti-racism, feminism, gay liberation, environmentalism, etc.) has been co-opted by and incorporated into the system.

My position is actually very similar to the position the Left faced in the 1960s when conventional blue collar workers and union types had largely been incorporated into the middle class, and maintained a pro-imperialist position on Vietnam, so the Left had to look elsewhere to build the antiwar movement.

> *"The issue Preston takes up is if reactionary counter-cultural movements, from neo-Nazis to Mormon Fundamentalists, can be united to challenge the global hegemony of capitalist power. The reality is that with visions so radically different, as well as analysis about power and oppression so different, they hold little tactical or ideological virtue in each other. Simply put: we don't want the same things, and even in challenging the state we would engage with it in such radically different ways that we do not hold stake in each other's success."*

Since National-Anarchism seems to be the real sticking point for these folks, here are some examples of how actual N-As describe their philosophy:

On the flags of nations and regions:

> *"Not participating in this group while they have their flags of the French State in their profiles. Solidarity of NAM of course with the Parisian people not with its state flag."*

> *"I think in many cases flags, although still official symbols of States, have become symbols of the people in some way, since several of them have been around for a long time and have gone hand in hand with the representation of peoples and their culture, not just the State/government."*

> *"What about regional flags, like the flags of Brittany, Galicia, Euskal Herria and the like, though? Would they not be considered symbols of the State too? And if so, are there any flags that are genuine symbols of the people?"*

> *"I think the anarchist black flag will do just fine…"*

> *"The problem I see with that is that that flag might represent people, but not their individual culture/area. I think that regional flags would do just fine, since they can be more closely related to a community/nation/folk than the national flag (regional/provincial flags will have more symbols referring to the local culture), and their "political meaning" is minimal most times."*

"Some flags can represent a cool story even if it represents a state. Like the flag of Bangladesh, it's green with a red circle in the middle. The green represents vegetation since it's a tropical biome. The red represents blood because it's liberation cost 3 million civilian lives over the course of 9 months."

"I consider my flag to be the black flag of anarchism, and I consider all the flags of the hyphenated anarchist tendencies to represent the many sects and tribes within anarchism. I also appreciate the way some anarchists will superimpose an anarchist symbol on particular national flags."

On Rojava:

"A nation fighting a nation-state. They are cosmopolitan and not multicultural. They have forged their own culture on top of their traditional culture, and any visitors or residents need to respect that culture or keep moving on to anywhere which tolerates sexual, religious or cultural domination or conflict. House rules are specified on entry, so your culture will be respected IF it adapts to the culture of your host."

On American gun culture:

"I loathe the gun culture in countries like America, but there is clearly a difference between being a gun-toting psychopath and having a weapon for defense. As the old saying goes, in a society without guns only the criminals will have guns. If I had a button that could instantly make all guns disappear, I would be very tempted to press it. At the same time, if I lived in a place like America then I would feel the need to get a gun for defensive purposes, just to give myself as much of a fighting chance as anyone else. That's the problem, you see, it's much like civilisation. People are travelling in a perpetually linear direction – upwards and onwards, never back – that has led them to become slaves to modern society and all the destruction that it brings."

"I really wish gun culture in America wasn't so entrenched in neocon dogma."

"I admire the roots of American gun culture, as it has its basis in self-reliance and personal responsibility. Devoid of any community cohesion, however, it becomes misanthropic and borderline

psychopathic. Having said that, I would far prefer living amongst an armed populace rather than one which had been disarmed and infantilised by the state "for our own good."

On racism:

"Although I don't support separatism (sic), it will be a preference of many productive people, and Anarchism not answering that question in the past, resulted in many non-racist people supporting fascists. If the people move forward with what they know, then PC black people should be allowed to have their safe spaces, which would make Martin Luther King turn in his grave, since he fought against such segregation. Since many are still referred to as "you people", they might find it more comfortable operating in spaces where black people who identify with their experience come together, while the rest remain in multi-ethnic communities. The same would apply to white people, Asians who are still discriminated against, etc. When things stabilize in the absence of these state pressures, people will start coming together more freely."

"Europe has always identified itself on a ethnic basis, rather than a racial one."

"To me it seems the purely racial view is more associated with the multiculturalism of the new world. So maybe with the watering down of European individuality because of modern multiculturalism, it only makes sense these ideas find their way here. But to me it presents an alienated idea, that developed in a alienated culture (or rather a lack of culture) to begin with."

" I believe that even if someone is mixed they should be proud of who and what they are."

"What I think is far more important than knowing how many people prefer to live among people of their own ethnical and cultural background is that in N-AM there is mutual respect and open communication between those individuals and groups who choose to live on way or another. In that we are all "equal". That is something hard to fathom for the anti-N-AM crowd who prefer uniformity on all levels."

"The nation needs anarchism as its only certainty for an equal and just society and economy for its people. Anarchism needs the

nation for its sense of community and to respond to the ever more encroaching globalism."

"It's something of a paradoxical question. I get asked about this all the time by leftists who are wondering if N-A really is a form of fascism, white supremacy, KKKism, etc etc etc, and by rightists who want to know the difference between N-A and the leftist/PC/SJW anarchists. I usually respond by saying I can only express my own views and that it's not my place to speak for N-As as a tendency. I explain that I consider myself a pluralistic or "pan" anarchist, and that I'm interested in all forms of anarchism, libertarianism, decentralism, or anti-statism. I consider N-A to certainly be a legitimate form of anarchism, and one that emphasizes racial, cultural, and ethnic identity, including white or European forms of identity, to be a preferred form of anarchism, or the most practical form of anarchism, or their individual or their own group's form of anarchism, depending on the individual and group in question. This concept could just as easily apply to black, brown, red, or yellow anarchists as well as white ones, and among ethno-cultural identities (Irish, Basque, Dutch, Alawite, Ibo, Maori, Hmong, Cherokee, etc) identities as much as the broader racial ones (European, African, Asian, Arab, Native American, etc. and variations among these). But N-A is also non-universalist in that it recognizes the legitimacy of non-European or non-white forms of identitarianism, as well as mixed or multicultural or "liberal" communities or whatever. So N-A ends up overlapping with other philosophies like pan-anarchism, anarchism without adjectives, and anarcho-libertarianism from the anarchist milieu, and concepts like ethno-pluralism, and pan-nationalism from ordinary nationalist or identitarian milieus.

The question of actual "racial separatism" comes down to being a matter of individual or group practice, regardless of the race or ethnic group in question, and the question of "racial supremacy" is kind of like the question of whether someone believes their religion is superior to others, i.e. it's matter of institutional cultural, organizational, community, or individual practice and belief. Do some white or European N-As believe their racial or ethnic group is superior? Perhaps. Just like some Christian N-As might think their Church is the true, or most true, Church, or their preferred economic system is the best one as well."

"Skin color differences doesn't mean you can't ever share a national identity or cultural values. Historically and even currently such as in Rojava anarchism with nationalist tendencies didn't advocate racial separatism."

"What I like about N.A. is that your nation or tribe is whatever you want. You have more traditional identities like Chinese, Muslim, American, etc. You can have more personal ones too like Jedi, Anime Freak, Skater, Metal-Head, etc. If you have enough people of the same identity, they can be a nation or tribe. That's what I like most about National Anarchism. There's more respect from N.A. regarding subcultures as potential tribes than anywhere else. I mean, aren't all identities artificial constructs anyway?"

"I think that defining the Nation by cultural values, rather than by differing ethnicities, is far more fruitful and sensible. This is extremely obvious in Europe, where in many Nations there isn't and has never been ethnic homogeneity (Germany and Finland are prime examples) and the feeling (or disbelief) of unity has been based on cultural and linguistic (among others) similarity instead. The European invention of Nation in the 19th century also didn't include racial ideas."

"Although I would prefer to live in a community of my own folk, I have always accepted that an Anarchist or NA community can be made up of what people you wish to be associated with! For the record I'm not a fan of Racial Nationalists who's idea of 'Nationalism' is to promote the state."

"As a black man (or whatever term being used these days smile emoticon), I am not a racial separatist myself but respect the right for others to want to do so. I feel that way strongly due to my personal experiences but my views are just my views. It doesn't mean it applies to others. What works for me may not work for someone else because personal experience ultimately determines what a person may feel about a particular situation. I have no problem working with National Anarchists of any sort, like the philosophy and consistency, and respect the way they want to live their lives. I have read your books many times and enjoyed them."

"I would like to see more Black people get involved in National-Anarchism, particularly in light of the great work that has already been done by the likes of Osiris Akkebala, Marcus Garvey, Louis Farrakhan and others. None of them Anarchist, of course, but certainly figures that have taken an enormous amount of pride in their identity and tried to do the best for their people."

"I would like to see more black people look at National Anarchism

also. I think it would be very fruitful. I know people who I think would be open to it once the ideas behind it was delivered clearly and succinctly."

"In my experience and research, the only people who do not want non-white individuals involved with National-Anarchism are the "Social Justice Warriors" within the politically correct totalitarian humanist authoritarian left circles involved with Antifa and groups like that."

"No one I'm aware of involved with N-AM has told me that non-white people are forbidden from being involved with National-Anarchism and I think it needs to be emphasized more so that it is our critics who are the ones who seek to prevent non-white people from participating in something that any group of people should be capable of contributing positive development toward."

"I see National Anarchism as a structure that can work no matter what your belief system is. Dogmas will occur but at the local level. The structure is dogma free. Every man or woman is a star. Every community is a galaxy with its own center be that an ideology or a person or a system."

On economics:

"Personally I would prefer not to start off a community with any set economic system in mind. Instead I would like to see my group's economy develop organically with the community members solving problems as they go. Whether it develops into something that could be considered Communist, Socialist, Distributist, or Capitalist doesn't really matter to me if it works for the community and does not adversely affect or impose upon other communities."

"Organic development is the key. Personally, though, my economic perspective owes more to Hoppe, von Mises and Rand than Douglas, Chesterton or Marx. That probably puts me at odds with the majority of folks on here, though."

"I'd personally like a Distributist model, but economics would need to come second to real-life issues. A self-sufficient community where economics would really be just a means to trade, barter, etc."

"Considering I believe economic and social relations are the foundation of our current opression, I'm opposed to Capitalism.

This because the State exists only to protect the existing social and economic contradictions. For me Capitalism and the State are pretty much the same thing, so I reject both, for the simple reason one cannot survive without the other."

"I believe we should have a society without a state or capitalism but I believe we should live in self sufficient community with decentralized nonprofit private organizations to supply certain stuff and do it yourself with the supplies given and instructions sort of thing with very minimal technology with electricity done in very diy way but I agree with… we should have a bit of trade sort of thing again."

"Agrarian/cottage industries. Craft. Family firms & farms. Co-ops. Profits within reason."

These comments are hardly consistent with AFN's claims that "The NA's themselves focus on racial identity as they are essentially anti-State nationalists, who maintain the same violent racism and misogyny that most neo-Nazis do."

"One thing that Preston mentions both in his last article and in much of his larger work is a critique of Political Correctness. He often joins in with the narrative that PC culture is the grand leviathan that controls the culture, which is ideologically pre-school in nature. The notion that liberal social norms are somehow equal to capitalism, the church, the communist party, or the corporation in different times and places is ridiculous."

I would actually disagree that PC has yet achieved the all-encompassing ideological power of the Church in the Middle Ages, Wahhabism in Saudi Arabia, or the Communist Party in the Soviet Union. But I will argue that it is the guiding ideology of the dominant political coalitions in Western countries.

"We want to add, however, that we also oppose things like Political Correctness and call-out culture."

That's good to hear.

"Much of what you lump together with contemporary anarchism or Marxism you bring over from mainstream liberalism, which are exactly many of the points at which the radical left breaks away."

The Tyranny of the Politically Correct

The anarchist wing of the far Left is a like a Plato's forms version of political correctness as evidenced by, for example, such tactics as "progressive stacking" or the obsession with gender pronouns, or incidents such as the attacks on figures such as Lierre Keith and Kristian Williams, or the skirmish between Crimethinc and Anarchist People of Color, to name but a few examples. It is true that there are forms of political correctness or totalitarian humanism that are more prevalent among liberals than the far Left (such as enthusiasms for gun control, neo-puritan anti-smoking crusades, anti-sex worker feminism, food policing, etc.)

> *"The reality is that racism is real, just as rates of job hiring, incarceration, police violence, and pretty much all areas of social life can be seen as disparate between whites and racial groups of color."*

Ironically, I'm often accused by right-wingers of being too critical of the cops, the legal system, and the prison-industrial complex. Take a look at the core documents on the ATS homepage. You will see a link to Lorenzo Ervin's "Anarchism and the Black Revolution" and Michelle Alexander's "The New Jim Crow." I think race issues involve a lot of complexities and competing dynamics on which reasonable people can disagree.

> *"Women are the victim of misogynist violence at rates so systemic that their own home is one of the most dangerous places they can be and pregnant women are more likely to die from homicide than in any other way. Rape, assault, and harassment are daily threats for non-male members of our society."*

Who besides criminals is actually in favor this?

> *When you stand with neo-fascist organizations (even though we are sure that you will dispute that description) you empower their revolutionary vision, one that necessitates our failure."*

Well, there are about as many ideologies present on the "alternative right" as there are individuals. Ask 10 different people on the alternative right about their position on a single issue and you will get 15 different opinions. In my associations with the alternative right, I've encountered traditional conservatives, free market libertarians, economic nationalists, populists, monarchists, anarchists, fascists, Nazis, Strasserites, distributists, right-wing Marxists, national-Bolsheviks, white nationalists, southern nationalists, black conservatives, white nationalist Jews, anti-Semites, self-proclaimed "radical centrists," self-proclaimed "alternative leftists," liberal racial realists, anti-immigration feminists, atheists, pagans, heathens, Satanists, Protestant evangelicals, Catholics, Orthodox Christians, Hindus, Muslims, advocates of the nuclear family, advocates of polygamy, gays, persons with varying degrees of Asian, Persian, Arab, Hispanic, or Native American ancestry, Holocaust-deniers, Holocaust-believers, pro-lifers, pro-choicers, pro-European Unionists, anti-European Unionist, city-statists, ethnostatists, proponents of a European Imperium, Eurasianists, anti-Eurasianists, pro-Zionists, anti-Zionists, pro-Putinists, anti-Putinists, pro-Americans, anti-Americans, etc. etc. etc. etc. In fact, it would be impossible to have an alternative right political party because there would be no agreement on common goals or objectives. About the only unifying thread on the alternative right is being "pro-Western" and "anti-PC."

If anything, ATS is an even broader project than the alternative right because we see the struggle in global terms and not merely in Euro-centric ones, because the many different tactical concepts we promote could theoretically be used by all kinds of resistance movements, and because the pan-decentralist alternatives that we propose to the Empire are broad enough to include an almost infinite variety of communities and identities, and this includes "the Civil Rights Movement, Radical Feminism, Radical Ecology, the anti-nuke movement, Animal Rights, and a whole other range of actual social movements that allowed anarchism this evolution" as much as it includes anything outside of the Left. To repeat, pan-anarchism, pan-secessionism, and pan-decentralism are neither the Southern Baptist Convention or Occupy Wall Street, nor the Frente Nacional or FEMEN, nor Hezbollah or the PKK. What we are advocating for is a kind of meta-political, meta-strategic, and meta-institutional paradigm that is over and above these kinds of particular identities, ideologies, or struggles.

19

The Argument from Atrocity

A commenter at AnarchistNews.Org offered this response to my latest exchange with Anti-Fascist News:

> I read it. I read through other things on that site. Yikes. It's really bizarre that a large portion of Preston's criticism of "left" anarchists (anarchists) is that they have a kind of selective amnesia for the atrocities of the left (yeah duh). However we then are treated to this gem
>
> "In my associations with the alternative right, I've encountered traditional conservatives, free market libertarians, economic nationalists, populists, monarchists, anarchists, fascists, Nazis, Strasserites, distributists, right-wing Marxists, national-Bolsheviks, white nationalists, southern nationalists, black conservatives, white nationalist Jews, anti-Semites, self-proclaimed "radical centrists," self-proclaimed "alternative leftists," liberal racial realists," (this goes on and on)
>
> One certainly has to wonder why intentionally associating oneself with people who actively wish to recreate many of the past centuries atrocities is acceptable given his other arguments. If the left popular front has been disastrous for anarchists, the right popular front seems even worse.

This response certainly raises some valid points, though I think it misunderstands my arguments a bit.

The whole point of the statement from me that the commenter cites is to suggest there is no popular front among the "alternative right" due to a lack of a consistent philosophy or common goals. It's much like the Left in the sense of being mostly a reactive (in the sense of opposing social trends such as mass immigration or the entrenchment of PC) rather than a visionary set of tendencies (at least on the collective level - individuals may have their own visions). Based on my many discussions with participants in the alternative right about what kinds of government, economics, laws, cultural norms, foreign policy, organizational structures, strategic approaches, etc. they prefer I have received widely divergent responses.

But what I have found is that the "argument from atrocity" is just as prevalent on the Right as it is on the Left and vice versa.

The Left will raise the specter of the horrors of Nazism, Mussolini, Franco, Pinochet, right-wing military dictatorships, the Spanish Inquisition, the Ku Klux Klan, racist terrorists like Dylan Roof, hate crimes against minorities, abortion clinic bombers, police brutality, etc. etc. etc. etc. The Right will raise the specter of the horrors of Stalism, Maoism, Pol Potism, the Kim dynasty, the Reign of Terror during the French Revolution, atrocities on the Republican side during the Spanish Civil War, the high rates of violent crime in minority communities, Islamist terrorism, etc. etc. etc. etc. It's not like the world is divided into a perfect break between anarchists on one side and Stalinists or Hitlerites on the other.

The spectrum of statism, centralism, authoritarianism, etc. is more like a continuum. If Kim Jong-Un is a 0 and Max Stirner is a 100, then most nations would probably be in the 30-70 range. But the range between 70-100 is still pretty vast. We could start with Stirnerites at 100, then an-caps and an-coms, then minarchists and syndicalists, then classical liberals and libertarian socialists, then paleocons and the ACLU, etc.

On the 0 end, there could be Hitler, Stalin, Mao, Pol Pot, and the Kims. Figures like Saddam Hussein, Castro, Ho, Robert Mugabe, Qadaffi, the Assads, Mussolini, Franco, Nasser, Peron, Chavez, etc. would be at various points in the authoritarian range. Conventional, mainstream Western liberal center-left and center-right politicians would mostly be somewhere in the middle (with lots of variations, outliers and fluctuations).

The ambition here is to cultivate a new opposition that rejects the emerging ruling class paradigm of therapeutic-managerial statism, neoliberal economics, liberal internationalist or "human rights" imperialism, and *de facto* "totalitarian humanism" as its legitimating ideology. This would be a new paradigm that is in opposition to the emerging dominant paradigm, and whose component parts would be the various philosophies, movements, and issues described in the ATS statement of purpose, among others.

The Tyranny of the Politically Correct

Some parts of this new paradigm would be primarily concerned with statism for different reasons, some with neoliberalism, some with imperialism, some with totalitarian humanism, and some with single issues or the perceived interests of their own reference groups. The cultivation of this paradigm plus the strategic ideas we promote provides the means for self-determination for all sorts of cultural and political factions in ways that do not require an overarching state apparatus.

At one point, anarchists were a large international radical movement. Anarchists were larger than the Marxists at one point, and held sizable minorities in a number of countries. I think the main difficulty anarchists of that time had was that they were swimming against the tide. The 20th century was the century of ever more centralized and bureaucratic institutions, not to mention total war. But now things are starting to go the other way (see the work of Martin Van Creveld on this question).

During the Spanish Civil War, anarchists managed to organize a popular front against the ruling class of the time. There's no reason these models can't be replicated at some point in the future, although anarchist theory has to be modified to fit contemporary societies. For instance, the dogmatic anarcho-communism and anti-clericalism of the Spanish anarchists certainly isn't appropriate for the present time in the Western world. But many other aspects of historic anarchism certainly are, and our model of decentralized, pluralistic, particularism provides us with an opportunity to connect with folks all over the political and cultural spectrum.

The views we promote here shouldn't be that difficult to understand. We promote pan-secessionism as a strategy on the model suggested by Kirkpatrick Sale. From there it's Freetown Christiania for leftists, and Orania for rightists, Mondragon for an-syns, kibbutzim for an-coms, and Liechtenstein for an-caps.

To the degree that movements from either the far Right or the far Left embrace the paradigm outlined above they are compatible with the ATS philosophy. To the degree they reject the above paradigm, the more they are incompatible. It's really pretty simple.

20

The Legacy of Anarchist Successes?

A commenter at AnarchistNews.Org posting as "SirEinzige" offers these observations concerning yours truly and my previous reply to a commenter on the same thread:

> "What Preston doesn't seem to realize is that classical anarchist failures were to an inherent degree rooted in their organizational successes which played a role in things like the new deal..., " "Also, Stirner is not on the ideology scale and certainly nowhere near an-caps."

There's a lot of substance in this short statement that is worth addressing. The first point involves an assessment of the relative successes and failures of the anarchist wing of the historic labor movement.

> "classical anarchist failures were to an inherent degree rooted in their organizational successes which played a role in things like the new deal."

This comment is actually reminiscent of something I wrote 15 years ago lamenting the drift of much of anarchism into implicit social democratic reformism.

> "The reality of course is that anarchism was one of the most successful mass movements ever. Yes, the state has yet to be abolished. No nation to date has adopted the black flag as its own. Yes, the international bourgeoisie retain their power. Class rule is with us now as much as ever. However, when we look at the state of things in the industrialized world a century ago we see that history has indeed moved in our direction.
>
> Anarchists were at the forefront of the movement for the eight-hour workday. The Haymarket martyrs gave their lives for this cause. At one point it was illegal to organize labor unions. Striking workers were regularly gunned down by government agents and private thugs.

171

It was a federal crime in the United States to distribute information about contraception. Orphaned children were confined to slave-like conditions and used for medical experimentation along with the mentally handicapped, juvenile delinquents, homosexuals and others. Prison conditions often rivaled those of Nazi concentration camps. The death penalty was regularly imposed for burglary and grand larceny. People of African descent were regularly murdered and terrorized by gangs of racists while authorities looked the other way.

Anarchists were among the earliest and most militant opponents of all of these conditions. The eight-hour day, the right to organize unions, read sexually explicit literature, practice contraception and obtain abortions and engage in antiwar protests, prison reform and countless other rights and privileges that we take for granted today did not exist at the time of the classical anarchist movement. Roger Baldwin was inspired to found the American Civil Liberties Union after hearing a speech by the anarchist and pioneer womens' rights advocate Emma Goldman. Anarchists were among the earliest opponents of the mistreatment of homosexuals as well. In many ways, things have advanced considerably over the past century."

In other words, while the classical anarchist movement failed miserably to actual carry out revolutions against states and ruling classes, many of the issues and ideals championed by the movement were eventually realized to at least a partial degree.

SirEinzige appears to be arguing that the actual successes of anarchist labor organizing efforts proved to be their undoing at the end of the day, because the labor movement that the anarchists helped to organize subsequently grew to the point where A) it actually achieved comprehensive labor reforms that ironically undermined the general militancy of the labor movement and B) allowed for the cooptation of the labor movement under the New Deal compact. It could be argued a similar narrative unfolded in other industrialized nations as well during the same era.

But this observation folds into the New Left recognition that the industrial proletariat in Western capitalist countries had ceased to be a revolutionary or even oppositional force due to rising living standards, technological innovation, the growth of consumer culture, the integration of the industrial working class into the middle class, the integration of labor and social democratic parties into the state, the institutionalization of labor unions, a range of political, legal, and economic reforms, etc.

In fact, by the 1960s workers in advanced industrialized nations had largely become a conservative force. Hence, the "workerist" orientation that continues to be championed by our classical syndicalist and libertarian communist friends became obsolete.

I was a "workerist" myself during my early years as an anarchist (1980s), and even held offices in classical syndicalist organizations like Workers Solidarity Alliance and the Industrial Workers of the World. My rationale for this position was pretty shallow as it amounted to little more than "because that's how they did it in the classical anarchist movement." But I was zealous for this perspective and worked as a strike support volunteer for a number of major strikes that were going on at the time.

Now, obviously new challenges have arisen for the working class due to the rise of neo-liberalism and globalization since the 1970s, and I still regard aspects of classical syndicalism and anarcho-communism to be relevant to contemporary economics. The syndicalist model of industrial organization advocated by economists such as Diego Abad de Santillan (see Mondragon for a partial example) or the anarcho-communist communes advocated by Kropotkin would continue to seem to be just as legitimate as any other kind of economic arrangements. Prototypes for these exist in the form of things like intentional communities, eco-villages, the kibbutzim, etc. I even think classical syndicalism as a tactical approach might continue to be relevant to societies that are in earlier stages of economic development (i..e the periphery).

But the real challenge when it comes to labor organization in a society like the United States concerns how to go about doing so in an economy heavily dominated by part-time service industry workers in transient jobs and highly skilled technical workers, where outsourcing is an ongoing reality, where intra-class stratification among the working class is increasingly prevalent, and where nearly 90 percent of the workforce is non-unionized.

"At most his focus should be tertiary with no strange bedfellows and separate means and ends. In that regard, secession could have a place in anarchist tactics but to the point of becoming part of the machine of organization, positions and solutions."

173

The Legacy of Anarchist Successes?

The question of "strange bedfellows" and "separate means and ends" raises issues of what the ranking of strategic priorities should necessarily be. My general observation has been that the bulk of the anarchist milieu in the Western countries, particularly in the United States, along with the "general left" as well, is principally oriented towards the advancement of cultural politics, identity politics, and issues of a social or cultural nature, rather than issues pertaining to imperialism, international relations, geopolitics, and the state itself, with even class issues playing second fiddle to cultural politics.

I have argued for a reversal of this ranking of priorities in almost an exact order whereby opposition to the Empire, American imperialism, and imperialism generally would be the primary focus (this is particularly important for those of us who are residents or citizens of the United States, the world's leading imperialist regime). The secondary focus would be opposition to the state (again, a particularly important focus given the growth of the surveillance state, the police state, and the prison-industrial complex). The tertiary focus would be on economic questions as these issues impact the greatest number of people in the wider society, irrespective of identity issues. The quaternary focus would be on preferred sets of economic arrangements, lifestyle preferences, favored identity groups, and favored social issues. At present, the majority of the anarchist milieu appears to be primarily oriented towards the quaternary category to the detriment of the first three categories. However, this does not mean that there should not be secondary organizations that are specifically oriented towards "preferred sets of economic arrangements, lifestyle preferences, favored identity groups, and favored social issues." In fact, I think such organizations would be among the foundations for the development of alternative infrastructure on the fourth generation warfare model (see Hezbollah). I do think that the anarchist milieu frequently exhibits certain excesses and imbalances in these areas as well, but that's a separate argument.

Regarding the issue of "strange bedfellows," different sets of bedfellows are appropriate in different circumstances, and I have noticed that many if not most anarchists have a deeply ingrained habit of thinking in ideological rather than tactical terms. For example, many anarchists appear to be looking to gain ideological converts or persuading people to embrace a certain social, cultural, moral or ethical vision in an almost quasi-religious sense (e.g., "Whitey must repent of the sin of racism and come to accept the egalitarian gospel.") This would seem to be an impractical approach. Rather, the ambition should be less focus on ideological and moral conversion and more on building coalitions around practical goals.

For example, if fast food or superstore workers go out on a general strike, obviously such an effort has to be inclusive of all workers in such industries regardless of not only their identity affiliations but also their wider cultural or political affiliations. It would not be appropriate to expect all participants in such an action to hold to a particular position on animal rights or gay marriage, for example.

Opposition to U.S. imperialism must by nature include, well, all opponents of U.S. imperialism, regardless of their views on other issues. For example, some of the best critiques of and efforts against U.S. imperialism originate from paleoconservative and libertarian-oriented Right.

The same is true of efforts against the state. As Larry Gambone puts it *"This must be a single issue movement, uniting everyone with a grievance against the state into a movement for the decentralization of power. It must not be allowed to be bogged down by secondary and therefore divisive issues. These can be dealt with by other groups."* Secession is merely a means towards this particular end.

As for the question of "organization, positions and solutions," we at American Revolutionary Vanguard and Attack the System have produced a wide range of material on these questions, as a cursory examination of our website will indicate. Of course, others may disagree with many of our views, and that's fine, but we can hardly be accused of offering no ideas on such questions.

Lastly, on the issue of how to interpret Max Stirner, I agree his ideas transcend ordinary political ideologies, and that Stirner's individualism is far more radical than that of the anarcho-capitalists (as even Rothbard admitted). But that's my point. Stirner's ideas represent an almost metaphysical characterization of human freedom in all of its paradoxes, and his complete negation of all institutions and ideologies places him at the top of the anarchist heap.

21

Left Only, or Beyond Left and Right?

What follows is the transcript of a debate that I had on this question with a left-anarchist/libertarian socialist on a social media forum.

A defence of anarchism as (1) libertarian socialism, and (2) an anti-hierarchical and inclusive philosophy of society. Any set of ideas which permits hierarchies of power or exclusion of people based on nationhood, race, gender, or sexuality is categorically not anarchist – despite what they may call themselves.

This includes laughable ideologies such as "anarcho"-capitalism and national-anarchism; both promoted by effing lunatic Keith Preston of Attack the System.

Personally I don't see why you even feel the need to self-identify as an anarchist. This "pan-secessionist" stuff is clearly a different thing altogether.

Anarchism is the underlying philosophy and ideological backdrop. Pan-secessionism is merely a tactical concept (like a general strike, an electoral campaign, or guerrilla insurgency).

The problem is what it seeks to create with that "tactic" isn't anarchism (voluntary non-hierarchy), but a bunch of smaller forms of archism, with some actual forms of anarchism among them.

The idea is to overthrow imperialism, capitalism, and overarching states by means of dissolution. The universal triumph of pure anarchism is a much broader and longer term project. A more intermediate objective is the forging of a society-wide pan-decentralist consensus rooted in the principle of self-determination for all.

The various forms of monarchism, racial separatism, and capitalism promoted don't exactly further self-determination by those who bear the brunt of them.

You're assuming that all people everywhere prefer libertarian values for themselves, and they clearly don't. Compulsory anarchism hardly seems anarchistic. For example, there are some in the Hawaiian independence movement who wish to restore their traditional monarchy that existed before the US invasion in the late 19th century. I would say that is a decision for the Hawaiians to make for themselves. Racial separatism is a prevalent undercurrent in African-American self-determination movements. Again, that is a decision for the parties involved to make for themselves. "Capitalism" is an elastic concept. I don't find all forms of capitalism to be inherently objectionable even from an anarchist point of view. There's a difference between good Lysander Spooner individualists and the Ayn Rand cult, for example, and still more difference between even vulgar an-caps and state-capitalist plutocrats. It's the same way "communism" spans the spectrum from intentional communities and hippie communes to more formalized collectives like the kibbutzim to the government of Cuba.

> *"Self-determination" in the broad sense you describe is not a good thing. I don't see the point of achieving some kind of formal liberation from a centralized/hierarchical power-structure if what replaces it is merely another such power-structure but on a smaller scale.*

Maybe that smaller scale makes it slightly less bad. That's largely immaterial. The point is the overthrow of the global plutocratic super class which has managed to centralize control over wealth on an unprecedented scale. About 150 corporations now dominate the world's economy. Some of these have more wealth and power than individual nation-states. The other big issue is the need to overthrow the American imperialist empire which now has unprecedented military and cultural power resulting in the infliction of death and suffering on peoples all over the world not to mention the imposition of a cultural homogenization.

> *"Even if one were to adopt the ethic "whatever they choose for themselves I'll accept." that wouldn't mean anarchists should support it AS ANARCHISTS."*

Self-determination has to be a principle of anarchism. Otherwise we merely become "anarcho-imperialists." Self-determination does not imply uncritical acceptance but merely respect for authentic diversity even if one is inclined to disagree.

*"The question should not be "is it less bad than what we have now?",
but "does it further the dissolution of hierarchical power and the
values of decentralism, mutual aid, and unity-in-diversity."*

Both are important. It's not a question of either/or. Indeed, I would
argue that the tactical concepts of "pan-secessionism" and other ideas
our camp promotes are means towards such ends as "decentralism,
mutual aid, and unity-in-diversity." All three of these concepts are at
the heart of our position at Attack the System.

*"Many of the little archies being supported are in fact a step
backwards in that regard."*

That's a rather bold claim. The idea that the possibility of, say, the
proliferation of communes representing "conservative" values, such
as religious monasteries and ethno-centric communes, is a regression
from global capitalism and liberal imperialism would seem to be a
rather myopic perspective.

*To use your own words, it's not an either/or. We shouldn't have to
choose between throwing our lot in with racists and religious lunatics
on one hand and the global neoliberal superstate on the other.*

*This however, is something qualitatively different: the method is
simply tactical alliances of the enemy's-enemy-is-my-friend kind
with those who not only have zero commitment to a voluntary non-
hierarchical society, but would find such a thing repugnant.*

*Even if an anarchist would see tons of smaller archies outside the
global neoliberal superstate as a means-to-an-end – with the final
goal being a genuine voluntary, non-hierarchical, cooperative
order covering the whole planet – MOST of those smaller archies
themselves would not see it that way. They would view their
monarchies, racial supremacist enclaves, religious communes as
permanent fixtures with no aspiration to move in the direction of an
inclusive/horizontalist society. Meaning actual anarchists are back
to square one.*

*With the popular classes still subordinate to a propertied elite in
much the same way as before – having to carve out little spaces
of freedom and equality within the capitalist death-machine and
according to their rules.*

Left Only, or Beyond Left and Right?

I think you're overemphasizing that aspect of our approach to a great a degree. Considerations of that type are maybe one percent of our overall strategy. The general trend worldwide, or at least in the core, has been towards greater cultural liberalization. The existence of the reactionary tendencies that you describe merely represents a reaction to those trends. Meanwhile, the development of a firm oppositional stance by such sectors can only have the effect of weakening the overall grip of the overarching neoliberal system. Lastly, the more objectionable certain cultural, political, or demographic sectors are, the better it is that they develop a decentralist and separatist outlook (i.e. mutual self-separation).

"I can see the logic of anarchists working WITHIN diverse struggles oriented around, say, national liberation, but only to try to push them in a more anarchistic direction."

Yes and the first struggle of that type is against the neoliberal international capitalist order, and the American imperialist empire.

"This is placing too much focus on opposing what exists now (on a global scale) and not enough on building what should exist (on a local scale).

"Anarchism, as a method, has always been about teasing out what libertarian elements are already latent within a given situation/ culture/idea-set, trying to push them to the forefront and make them predominant."

Yes, exactly. That's what our perspective is all about, i.e. attempting to push the anarchistic, libertarian, decentralist, anti-statist, anti-imperialist, or anti-authoritarian tendencies within all movements, subcultures, demographics, etc., to the forefront, and towards the purpose of developing a society wide consensus, however imperfect or incomplete, towards such ends.

"Even if an anarchist would see tons of smaller archies outside the global neoliberal superstate as a means-to-an-end – with the final goal being a genuine voluntary, non-hierarchical, cooperative order covering he whole planet – MOST of those smaller archies themselves would not see it that way. They would view their monarchies, racial supremacist enclaves, religious communes as permanent fixtures with no aspiration to move in the direction of an inclusive/ horizontalist society."

180

Again, we're talking about a continuum, not a zero sum game. The adoption of, for example, decentralism or mutual aid or "unity in diversity" as a tactical concept rather than a principled one by a wide range of otherwise "conservative" sectors still furthers the interests of decentralism, mutual aid, and unity in diversity, although in a de facto rather than de jour sense.

But an order has been established in such a scenario where power is more dispersed and where cracks of freedom are better able to grow and be cultivated. This is how the scientific revolution, the Renaissance, and the Enlightenment eventually emerged from the otherwise static order of the Middle Ages.

> *This is especially the case with "voluntaryist" proposals involving "private defense agencies". (States which they refuse to acknowledge as states)"*

I agree the theory behind PDAs is potentially problematic. I've had debates about that with an-caps actually. But again, we're talking about a spectrum. Anarchist militias of the kind favored by many an-coms and an-syns, for example, are also a kind of de facto PDA.

> *That's the problem I see with your approach, some ideologies have ZERO libertarian/decentralist/mutualistic tendencies latent within them to be developed into something more anti-authoritarian and inclusive.*

Monarchism, racial separatism, capitalism, etc. are such ideologies.

Cooperation with democratic socialists who aren't fully libertarian socialists makes sense from a tactical perspective. They are easiest to push in a decentralist and liberatory direction. This is not the case with racists and religionists and capitalists who seem superficially to have a decentralist thrust, but are only truly decentralist with regard to the existing global neoliberal superstate.

> *"With the popular classes still subordinate to a propertied elite in much the same way as before – having to carve out little spaces of freedom and equality within the capitalist death-machine and according to their rules."*

The plutocracy doesn't exist independently of the state. We've published a range of material about this in the past. I even wrote an award-winning essay on this question at one point. The question is one of concentrated versus dispersed power: political, economic, social, legal, military, etc.

> *"This is placing too much focus on opposing what exists now (on a global scale) and not enough on building what should exist (on a local scale)."*

Again, this is a false dichotomy. The objective is to develop tactical concepts like pan-secessionism while simultaneously cultivating localized struggles against local power elites. For example, in the US, while we're building pan-secessionism to overthrow the American empire and US federal government we also need to work on taking down the municipal governments of the major cities which are centers of the police state and crony-capitalism.

> *"This is looking at it in too simple a way. Certain forms of dispersed (but still authoritarian) power can in fact be harder to fight, and more difficult to carve out freedom from, than more formally centralized structures of rule."*

> *"Takis Fotopoulos supports something similar: arguing that libertarian socialism cannot be achieved until all countries pull out of the neoliberal order and regain economic and political/cultural self-reliance – which he sees as the material and social basis for building libertarian socialism in the long term."*

> *"The problem is that he seeks to do so by forming – as an intermediate stage – a second global "pole" to the neoliberal order called the "Eurasian Union" centered around Russia (which he holds has the material capacity to achieve self-reliance very quickly) and all other nations opposed to neoliberalism."*

> *"The problem is that this could – for the majority of those affected – wind up just as authoritarian, if not more so, than what exists now, if theocratic statists, state socialists, or other totalitarians managed to use it as a vehicle for their respective ideologies."*

> *"Pan-secessionism has similar problems. Even if ideally used as a vehicle, long-term, for creating anarchism, it would most likely be used to create newer forms of authoritarianism."*

> *"This however, is something qualitatively different: the method is*

simply tactical alliances of the enemy's-enemy-is-my-friend kind with those who not only have zero commitment to a voluntary non-hierarchical society, but would find such a thing repugnant."

I am not familiar with Fotopoulos although I am aware of this general theory which, while imperfect and not without its problematic aspects, does indeed represent a blueprint for a more multipolar order which as the very least would have the effect of further fracturing the international capitalist forces.

"An alternative approach I would recommend (which will be outlined more fully in a book I'm writing) is the creation of a two-tier international alliance of (1) left-wing nation-states opposed to neoliberalism and G7 dominance, and (2) explicitly libertarian socialist/anarchist confederations such as the Zapatista municipalities and Rojava cantons – and hopefully other such examples."

That sounds interesting. I will certainly have to read your book when it comes out. However, comparable dangers are present, such as the cooptation of the confederations you mention by the nation-states you describe, which has been a major part of the history of the Left in Western countries (i.e. popular movements with libertarian thrust being coopted by social democratic and neoliberal parties), and the re-direction of such movements towards explicit authoritarianism (see the entire history of the relationship of the libertarian left with Leninism).

"Take for instance the Ottoman Empire. One of the most brutal and centralised examples of power in recent memory. But they also largely left certain populations alone, unmolested to a large extent."

I'd argue more for the model of the Holy Roman Empire, which as Voltaire is supposed to have said, was "neither holy, nor Roman, nor an empire."

"With the Empire's breakup into many scattered colonial states, power was more dispersed, but people suffered greater degrees of brutality and repression overall."

But that didn't involve any genuine decentralization or self-determination. It merely replaced the Ottoman empire with the European colonial empires, and it came about due to the defeat of the Ottomans in WWI.

"Same with the decentralized Taliban versus the U.S.-imposed centralized government in Afghanistan."

That's comparing apples and oranges. The Taliban were a direct outgrowth of the mujahedeen, a proxy army organized by the West and the Gulf States whose ideology and, often, personnel and leadership were imported into Afghanistan from Saudi Arabia.

"The very fact you used the term "crony-capitalism" indicates a belief in a form of capitalism that isn't crony."

It's a matter of semantics. I'm talking about the alliance of state and capital into the kind of plutocratic power elites that dominate modern liberal societies (see C. Wright Mills), not Tucker's individualist anarchism or Molinari's radical classical liberalism or "Manchester liberalism" or agorism. As I said before, the spectrum of market economics represents a continuum as does "communism."

Pan-secessionism really amounts to little more than a tacit agreement by contending political and cultural forces to stay out of each others' backyards while recognizing the existence of a common enemy.

16328386R00105

Printed in Great Britain
by Amazon